Asperger's Syndrome
Workplace Survival Guide

A NEUROTYPICAL'S SECRETS FOR SUCCESS

BARBARA A. BISSONNETTE
PRINCIPAL OF FORWARD MOTION COACHING

Asperger's Syndrome Workplace Survival Guide: A Neurotypical's Secrets for Success
Barbara A. Bissonnette, Certified Coach

Copyright © 2010 Barbara A. Bissonnette, Forward Motion Coaching

All rights reserved. No part of this book may be reproduced in any manner whatsoever without the written permission of the copyright holder, except in the case of brief quotations embodied in reviews, and the *Asperger's Syndrome Guide for Employers* in the Appendix, which may be photocopied for distribution to employers.

This book was printed and bound by E Print, Inc., Hudson, NH
Graphic design by Tracy Hedberg

Library of Congress Control Number: 2010915028

ISBN-10 0-61540-759-5
ISBN-13 978-0-615-40759-3

Barbara Bissonnette
Forward Motion Coaching
119 Adams Drive
Stow, MA 01775
978-298-5186
www.ForwardMotion.info

Books may be ordered online at www.ForwardMotion.info

Dedication

I would like to dedicate this book to my esteemed mentor and friend, Ellen H. Korin, who encouraged me to pursue a new career coaching individuals with Asperger's Syndrome.

I am grateful to my wonderful husband for his unflagging support, without which this book would not have been possible.

Last, and certainly not least, I offer my thanks to the men and women with Asperger's Syndrome for all that they have taught me about perseverance in the face of adversity.

Contents

CHAPTER ONE: INTRODUCTION
What Does It Take to Make It in the NT Workplace, Anyway?, page 1

    How to Use This Book to Develop and Make Changes, page 6

CHAPTER TWO
Choosing the Right Career and Getting Hired, page 8

    How to Conduct Thorough Career Research, page 10
    Informational Interviewing, page 15
    Assess Why You are Not Getting Hired, page 22
    Tips for Job Interviews, page 28

CHAPTER THREE
Communication Skills at Work, page 30

    Pragmatics, Central Coherence and Theory of Mind, page 32
    Making the Right First Impression, page 39
    Communicating with Body Language, page 41
    Small Talk: Key to Relationship Building, page 44
    Why You Need a Work Buddy, page 47
    How to Be a Team Player, page 50

CHAPTER FOUR
Managing Your Career, page 54

    Build on Your Strengths, page 55
    Why You Need to Network, page 58
    A Primer on Office Politics, page 64
    How to Handle Conflicts and Disagreements, page 72
    Feedback and Criticism, page 77
    Dealing with Authority, page 80

CHAPTER FIVE
Executive Functions at Work, page 83

    Working Memory and the Myth of Multitasking, page 84
    Project Planning, page 86
    The Importance of Flexibility and Processing Speed in Decision Making, page 87
    Three Simple Time Management Tips, page 91
    Asking for Help is a Good Thing; Being Too Helpful Is Not, page 93
    Meeting Employer Expectations, page 97
    The Importance of a Goal and a Plan, page 103

CHAPTER SIX
Workplace Disclosure, page 107

    How to Disclose in a Solution-Focused Way, page 111
    Examples of Disclosure Strategies, page 116

CHAPTER SEVEN
Managing Anxiety, Frustration, Anger and Stress, page 120

    How to Avoid Cognitive Distortions, page 123
    Changing Distorted Thinking Patterns, page 126
    Managing Anxiety, page 129
    Sensory Issues on the Job, page 132
    Dealing with Change, page 136
    What to Do If You Are Fired, page 140

CHAPTER EIGHT
In the Final Analysis, page 145

APPENDIX
Asperger's Syndrome Guide for Employers, page 148

BIBLIOGRAPHY, page 156

INDEX, page 159

CHAPTER ONE: INTRODUCTION

What Does It Take to Make It in the NT Workplace, Anyway?

I am not aware of any reliable employment statistics for adults with Asperger's Syndrome (AS). An often quoted statistic is that 85% are either un- or under-employed. Whether that number is accurate or not, clearly there are too many intelligent, college-educated individuals who are not able to fully utilize their talents in the workplace.

Kevin summed up a big part of the problem. He was crushed after losing his first post-college job in just six weeks. "At school it was about getting good grades," he said, "at work it's about figuring out what people want."

If you are a person who has Asperger's Syndrome, figuring out what people want probably seems like an impossible task. No matter how hard you try, you just don't "get it" like everyone else does. At work, people can say one thing but mean another. They accuse you of not listening, yet won't tell you exactly what they want from you. When you guess, you usually guess wrong.

It is exhausting to be anxious every day about saying or doing the wrong thing. You want to interact with your co-workers, but don't know what to say. Sometimes, their conversations seem so trivial or boring that you don't even try to join in. Other times, you think that you're being friendly and helpful but are accused of being "rude" or "hard to get along with." Why all the emphasis on socializing, anyway? What is more important: chatting in the lunch room or getting your work done?

Speaking of getting your work done, the continual interruptions make it so hard to concentrate! You lose track of what you were doing, or forget altogether. The pressure starts to mount. You're getting confused.

Soon, you become paralyzed. You are not sure what you should be doing, so you abandon the current project and return to an earlier task. Later, your supervisor says that you need to prioritize better.

On top of all this, you are assaulted by sights, sounds, smells and textures that are uncomfortable (even torturous) that no one else seems to notice. Why can't people turn down the lights, be quiet and stop eating noxious smelling food at their desks?

It is all very frustrating and sometimes makes you really angry, particularly if you have been fired once, or more than once, or many more times than once and you don't really know what went wrong before. What are you supposed to do differently now? It keeps getting harder to explain the employment gaps and short-term jobs on your resume. You shouldn't lie, but if you tell the full truth, no one will want to hire you.

Perhaps you are employed, but struggle to carry out job duties, or are bored in a position that doesn't make use of your intellect. Maybe you have earned a promotion where you are required to show "leadership" and have no idea what to do. Or, worst of all, a new supervisor has changed all the rules leaving you once again to frantically try and figure out what is expected of you now.

At times you wonder whether you should disclose your Asperger's Syndrome to your employer. Technically, the Americans with Disabilities Act protects people from discrimination, but this is the real world. It is hard to predict how your manager will react, and proving discrimination can be difficult, time consuming and expensive. Still, disclosure means that you can request accommodations, which you are certain would enable you to improve your performance dramatically.

If you can relate to any of the above, then you have a lot in common with the clients in my coaching practice. They are men and women who, like you, are smart and skilled. Most have college degrees, and some have master's degrees or doctorates. They are young people who are just entering the workforce, and they are people in their 30's, 40's, 50's and even 60's who have spent years at work in all kinds of careers.

Although they have been diagnosed with Asperger's Syndrome (or strongly suspect that they have it) each client is very different. For some, holding on to any job is an incredible challenge. Others maintain steady employment, and some get promoted, yet often struggle to understand expectations and communicate with co-workers. My clients include people who are working in major corporations, academic institutions or research facilities. There are entrepreneurs, medical and legal professionals, directors and vice presidents, and they still grapple with interpersonal skills.

My clients seek coaching to discover what career they will like and be successful at, to learn how to interview and to improve their communication skills. They want techniques for managing time better and prioritizing projects. They want to know how to address performance problems, decide whether or not to disclose, and learn how to disclose. All want to figure out just what it is that NTs want. (NT stands for neurotypical, meaning a person who is not on the autism spectrum.)

As an NT, I act as a bridge between my clients and the neurotypical workplace. Prior to coaching, I spent 20 years in the business world; managing departments, increasing sales, launching new products and hiring staff.

My introduction to Asperger's Syndrome happened by accident. In the spring of 2006, I was midway through a graduate certificate program in executive coaching from the Massachusetts School of Professional Psychology (MSPP). Four years earlier, I had quit my job as Vice President of Marketing and Sales, and then consulted part-time with that company, while testing the waters of professional coaching. I wanted to give back my business experience to people who could benefit the most from it. Coaching entrepreneurs and small business owners seemed the ideal way to do that.

Thumbing through the MSPP continuing education catalog, I noticed a workshop about coaching people with Asperger's Syndrome. It sounded interesting so I gave myself permission to take a Friday morning off to attend.

I spent the better part of four hours that Friday literally on the edge of my chair. What I heard was fascinating and familiar. I was certain that during my corporate career I had worked with people who had AS. A few weeks later, I met with the executive director of the Asperger's Association of New England. She asked a question that changed everything. "Have you thought about coaching people with Asperger's?"

Could I? I began my due diligence; reading books, visiting Web sites and talking to educators, advocates, psychotherapists and neuropsychologists. I attended workshops and conferences. I talked to more professionals. My idea was to specialize on career development coaching for Asperger's adults. It was met with universal enthusiasm. "No one is doing that," I heard again and again. Finally, I had found a group of people who could benefit from my business experience.

Today, I coach individual's with Asperger's Syndrome and Nonverbal Learning Disorder on a range of issues related to work and career. Sometimes, people contact me hoping that I hold a magic key or can suggest one particular activity that will clear the path for their career success. As I listen to their stories, I wish that there was a magic key, but there is not. The coaching process requires learning and practicing new skills, taking action toward a goal, and a willingness to experiment. Coaching is not about changing who you are as a person; it is about changing how you approach situations and interact with others, so that you can function more effectively at work. It can be about finding a job that capitalizes on your strengths, while discovering ways to minimize or work around your limitations.

In this book, you will learn about the techniques that I use with my clients. I'll share methods for avoiding misunderstandings with your co-workers, clarifying expectations with your supervisor and dealing with specific problems. Since I believe that it is easier to learn from examples, I have included many from my client cases. People's names and identifying details have been changed to protect their privacy, and in some cases composites have been used.

My perspective as a neurotypical business person will help you navigate confounding aspects of the workplace. Until the day when companies are "Aspie-friendly," the burden is on you to find ways to fit in. Even if you opt for self-employment, you will still interact with neurotypical customers, vendors or employees.

When I present a workshop, someone in the audience will ask why NTs are so "mean," or why Aspergian's are the ones who have to do all of the changing. "Just because I'm not a social person, it doesn't mean that I'm a bad person," one man said.

NTs aren't mean. But they are the majority. Most know little or nothing about Asperger's Syndrome. Despite the increased attention that AS has received from best-selling books, national magazines and television programs, the general population (including business people) still doesn't understand it. Myths and misconceptions abound. I still meet people who think that everyone with AS is a genius or is working in the information technology industry. Most believe the stereotype of the loner who "doesn't like people" and who isn't empathic. Some individuals think that Asperger's is a personality problem.

Within the workplace, the lack of understanding about AS means that communication gaffes are treated as attitude or behavior problems. Executive function difficulties are interpreted as lack of effort or caring. The individual having sensory issues is considered demanding and picky.

Should it be like this? No. Will it change overnight? No. Will it change someday? Yes. But what do you do in the meantime?

Choose a career wisely, based on your interests and strengths. Learn how to communicate *well enough* to get along with co-workers. Be open to new ways of doing things. Ask NTs for help (they are everywhere, so why not use them?!). Do not allow bad experiences from the past to make you angry and bitter. Instead think about how you want people to perceive you.

Remember, *everyone* has to fit into cultural expectations and norms. During my corporate career there were times that I had to work with people whom I didn't like, adhere to policies that I thought were silly, and settle for doing work that was good enough, instead of outstanding.

I experienced periods of boredom, uncertainty and frustration. I found some senior executives thoroughly intimidating. No job is perfect but you get a regular paycheck, health insurance, and paid vacation and sick time.

This is not to minimize in any way the very real challenges that the majority of people with Asperger's Syndrome face at work. It is to let you know that whenever groups of people get together, there will be conflicts, power struggles and frustrations. NTs have problems on the job, too.

How to Use This Book to Develop and Make Changes

The content of this book is based on the issues that I see again and again in my coaching practice. Not every chapter will apply to you, but many of them will. My intention is to provide specific actions and techniques that you can use to address various work situations. If you are just entering the workforce, this book will help you understand what employers expect from you and show you how to avoid some of the common problems that occur.

Choose one or two areas to focus on at a time. Trying to make too many changes at once is overwhelming and won't work very well. You might need help from a neurotypical who can translate some of the techniques into a plan that addresses your specific needs. This person can be a professional coach or psychotherapist or someone in your personal life who you trust. Perhaps there is a colleague at work you have a good relationship with who can help you put some of the ideas into action.

Action is the key when you want to make a change. Usually it is the small, consistent steps taken over time that get big results. You don't have to do everything perfectly, either. It takes practice to master a new skill. The most successful clients I work with are those who are willing practice new attitudes or behaviors, even though they initially feel uncomfortable. What they discover is that the more they do something, the more at ease they become with it.

Motivation is a factor when you are making changes. The best way to maintain your focus and determination over an extended period of time is to set a meaningful goal. When it comes to work, sometimes the big motivator for change is fear—usually of job loss. Even if this is your primary motivator, try to put it in the context of a larger, more positive goal. For instance, you may decide that your greater goal is to improve your communication skills, or ability to handle frustration, so that you are less likely to face the same kind of problem in the future.

Experiment with change. Decide what you will do differently, try it for a reasonable amount of time, and assess the results. Two to three weeks is often a realistic experimental period. Then, if the change isn't working, try something else.

Do not give up. I have worked with clients who tell me that they absolutely, positively, in no way, can never, ever, do something … and a few months later, they are doing it! If you find yourself becoming discouraged, seek out support. Difficulties in the workplace are not exclusive to people with Asperger's Syndrome. Plenty of NTs get fired, passed up for promotions, receive disciplinary actions or realize that they are in the wrong career. The key is to learn from your experiences and be willing to change.

CHAPTER TWO

Choosing the Right Career and Getting Hired

"It is critical for people with Asperger's Syndrome to take a fearlessly honest inventory of their strengths and challenges. This is important for anybody, but is especially crucial for those with AS who may have less social and emotional 'margin' for wrong turns."

Web Content Administrator, age 42

Success at work depends on many factors, including your interest in a particular field; whether you have the necessary talent, skills and education; the availability of jobs in your field; opportunities for advancement; the right work environment and being valued for your contribution. There is no shortage of books, Web sites, and assessments that provide vocational guidance. The problem is these tools are designed for neurotypical people.

I have coached individuals who work in all kinds of jobs, from entry-level positions to corporate executives with six-figure salaries. What I have found is:

- Interest in a subject doesn't necessarily mean that you will enjoy or be able to make a living in that field
- The environment you work in is as, or even more, important than specific job tasks
- Personal "eccentricities" are more often overlooked if you have skills that are in demand
- Careful research before investing in education can save you a lot of time, money and energy

One of my first clients was Michelle. Nearly a year after receiving her Bachelor's Degree in Early Childhood Education, she still had not found a job. She chose this major because the subject of human development was interesting, and because she liked to read to and play with children. Michelle realized during her college internships that working with preschoolers required more than reading and playing games. It was exhausting to keep track of the activities of several energetic three- and four-year-olds. Disciplining the children was difficult. The worst, though, was talking to parents when they came to drop off or retrieve their offspring. "I don't know what to say," Michelle admitted.

Michelle's social anxiety made it hard for her to talk to me during our coaching sessions. At job interviews, her tense facial expression and panicked exclamation of, "Oh my!" in response to questions that she didn't know how to answer made a poor impression. One daycare center manager advised Michelle to rethink a career working with young children.

Eventually, Michelle did just that, enrolling in a certificate program to train as a medical transcriptionist. The work offered structure and clear guidelines. Interpersonal communication would be limited to her co-workers.

It was only after Scott earned a Master's Degree in Anthropology that he realized how very few job openings there were in the field, and that most teaching positions require a doctorate. The entry-level jobs that he did get only lasted a few months. Scott was easily overwhelmed and needed explicit directions for every assignment. When stressed, he either became mentally paralyzed or made impulsive, poorly thought out decisions (he once hid in the men's room for 2 hours). When we first met he was working as a data entry clerk, frustrated to be using neither his intellect nor writing skills.

During our coaching sessions, we looked at Scott's interests. We also reviewed his limitations, which included problems multitasking, and high anxiety when confronted with unexpected situations. He decided to pursue technical writing because it would allow him to work alone for long periods of time on assignments that are highly structured in content, style and length.

Ed had spent nearly a decade in the legal profession. After

graduating cum laude from law school, he passed the bar exam on his first try and became an attorney at a small law firm. He was asked to resign after a few months, and quickly found work at another law office. Two years later, he was fired from this job, and then went on to hold 4 more positions that all ended in his being fired or asked to resign. In total, Ed had 6 different jobs over the course of 10 years.

Ed initially started coaching with the intention of finding yet another attorney's job. However after reviewing his career history, some telling patterns emerged. During his tenure at each firm, Ed did not socialize with his fellow attorneys, preferring to eat lunch by himself every day. His abrupt manner and refusal to follow office rules that he thought were "stupid" alienated him from the administrative personnel. The life-long discomfort Ed felt in social situations kept him from attending professional events, where he was expected to make new contacts. He lacked awareness of the cultural norms of a law firm. Once, he was reprimanded for stacking empty soda cans in his office.

As he described each job, a greater and greater fatigue seemed to engulf Ed. "Do you like practicing law?" I asked. "No," he admitted. His real love was research; his father had wanted him to be a lawyer.

We began exploring how he could transfer his research skills and writing ability to a career that would be more rewarding.

How to Conduct Thorough Career Research

Whether you are just entering the job market, are dissatisfied with your current career, or have repeatedly lost jobs in your current field, careful research increases the odds of finding the right match.

Evaluating your talents and skills is important. As a person with Asperger's Syndrome, it is also critical that you understand what your limitations are, so that you can avoid careers that would be frustrating or impossible for you to succeed at. Nearly all of the career advice in books and on Web sites is designed for neurotypical people. You will need to factor in any AS-related difficulties you have as you learn about different professions.

Rick was bored in his administrative job and wanted a career that was in line with his interests. His passion was baseball. "I'm 36 and know that I am way too old to play the game," he explained, "plus I'm not coordinated. What I want is a quiet, low-stress, behind-the-scenes job."

Initially, Rick's idea of a "behind-the-scenes" job was to manage team travel for a major league ball club. He based this choice on one detail: he wanted to work in an office, not amid the chaos of screaming fans in a stadium. It didn't take long for him to discover that managing team travel required a level of multitasking and deadline pressures that he simply couldn't handle.

Tasks are one part of a job. Another part is the work environment. I think that the environment is as or even more important than tasks if you are a person with Asperger's Syndrome. Your career research should include learning about what the environment is like in a particular industry. For example, start-up companies tend to operate under tight deadlines. There is a lot of pressure to ship products and make sales. Smaller staff means that individuals are responsible for a wider variety of tasks. You might not be able to keep up with the pace.

Individual companies also have their own environments, and this is usually referred to as a corporate culture. One firm might value efficiency and bottom-line results while another values creativity and innovation. Company A may reward collaboration and group results while Company B rewards individual accomplishment. Inquire about work environment during informational or job interviews. A good question to ask is, "How would you describe the ACME culture?" (Culture is discussed in detail in Chapter Four.)

The same job (e.g. systems manager) can be different depending on the company or industry. A corporate library, for example, will not be as hectic as a public library in a major metropolitan city. News reporters for daily papers write on shorter deadlines than feature writers at magazines. Serving customers at the post office involves a much more structured and predictable routine than serving customers at a busy restaurant.

Generally speaking, jobs at small companies are more horizontal.

That is, they involve a wider range of activities. Jobs at large companies tend to be more vertical. The work is more specialized and involves greater interaction with others.

Research the broadest range of occupations that will utilize your talents, skills and interests. Teachers, for example, can work in traditional classroom settings, and with children or adults. Corporate trainers work within corporations to teach employees about new systems or software. It is also a form of teaching to write instructional manuals and textbooks, or to develop curriculum or workshops. If you like animals, you might enjoy teaching canine obedience classes or training assistance animals.

Here is a four-step process that I use to help my clients research career options.

Step 1: *Develop a list of possible careers.* This exercise is worthwhile even if you think that you already know exactly what kind of occupation you want. Sometimes, what initially seems like the "perfect" career turns out to be undesirable. You may also discover appealing careers that you didn't even know existed, require less training, or are in greater demand.

A career interest inventory is useful if you have no idea what kind of work you might like, or if you can only think of two or three options. You answer a series of questions and receive a list of potential vocations based on your areas of interest. Some interest inventories are available at no charge online and others require a fee. Interest inventories do not measure a person's aptitude. You may not be suited for every potential career on the list. This is why thorough research is important.

Step 2: *Identify important work criteria.* Is it important that you have work that engages you intellectually? Or are job stability and low stress your "must have's?" Do you want to work in a large corporation with many possibilities for advancement, or is a small company with a "family" environment a better match? Do you enjoy traveling or do you prefer to go to the same place each day? Clarifying important criteria enables you to evaluate whether certain careers are a good match or not. To do this, create two columns on a sheet of paper. List your "must-have" job criteria in one column and the "nice to have" criteria in the other. The "nice to have" items are those that you are willing to compromise on if there are other positives that make a career appealing.

Here are examples of important career criteria that my clients have identified:
- salary range
- availability of work
- commuting time and cost
- creativity
- pace and deadlines
- structure and routine
- hours per week (overtime required?)
- type and amount of social interaction
- educational requirements
- benefits (including vacation and sick time)
- accessibility to public transportation

Step 3: *Conduct preliminary research.* Your list from Step 1 should contain at least five possible careers. The next phase of research is to learn all that you can about each one. You can research one career at a time, or several.

The Occupational Outlook Handbook (www.bls.gov/oco/) and O*Net (Occupational Information Network, http://online.onetcenter.org) describe of all kinds of jobs and careers, and include data such as educational requirements, salary range, projected job growth, related careers and more. The information on both of these Web sites is free.

Keep a separate file for each profession that you research. Write down what you find attractive about a career as well as what you are concerned about or dislike. As you progress with each stage of your research, grade your level of interest in a particular career. A grade of A/A- means that the work sounds interesting, and that you want to learn more. A grade of B/B- means that you have some concerns, but more information is needed. A grade of C/C- means that you are not interested in learning more at this time, but that you might decide to resume exploration in the future. The final grading level of D/F means "take it off the list!"

Posted job openings are another source for preliminary research. Search online job boards (e.g. Monster, Craigslist, etc.) and find at least five openings in the field that you are considering. Read through each posting, and write down the tasks that are emphasized, what skills are required, and the type of experience that the employer asks for.

What about teamwork, people skills and multitasking? These have become ubiquitous requirements and should not be the basis for ruling out a potential career. Teamwork, people skills and multitasking are general terms and can mean vastly different things, depending on a specific job, an industry, or even a particular company. At this stage of your research, unless there are other factors that make a profession unsuitable, do not put too much weight on these descriptors.

Step 4: *Conduct applied research.* After completing Step 3, most people have at least one career each on their "A," "B," and "C" and "D" lists. However, it can be difficult to imagine what a vocation will be like if you haven't experienced it. The next stage of career research helps you gain a more concrete understanding of what it would be like to work in a particular field.

There are several ways to conduct applied career research. Volunteering is an excellent option for gaining practical experience. It also offers a low pressure way to "ease in" to a work routine. If you are contemplating a career change, volunteering offers an opportunity to learn about different jobs and make some contacts in the field. Be strategic and select a volunteer opportunity that is related to your area of interest. You do not have to limit yourself to non-profit organizations. For example, if you want to work with animals, you can volunteer at a humane society, a veterinary office or at a grooming facility.

Professional associations often utilize volunteers to serve on committees. This is a good way to make industry contacts. The structured setting and shared interest of members makes it easier to initiate conversations and build relationships.

Job shadowing involves following someone at their place of employment as they go through their work day. It gives you first-hand exposure to a particular working environment. Job shadowing can take place over the course of an entire day or for two or three hours. The process for arranging a job shadowing experience is the same as for setting up informational interviews.

Informational Interviewing

Informational interviewing allows you to learn about a career by talking to people who are currently working in the field. It is not a job interview. You can ask questions about what the work is like, how to break into the field, what education is required and not, where the best opportunities are, and ask for the names of other people to contact. Many business people and professionals enjoy talking about what they do, and are willing to meet with individuals who are contemplating entering their field.

Generally, it is a good idea to speak with at least three different people within a profession. Their experiences will not be exactly alike, but patterns usually emerge. You might get confirmation that a career is an excellent match, or learn that you are unsuited for a certain field. The latter can save you a lot of time, money and frustration.

Appropriate questions to ask are those that will help you understand job tasks; the work environment; the skills, experience and education required; and facts about an industry. Inappropriate questions are those related to your job readiness, such as how to work as part of a team, how to make small talk or how to get organized.

There is a six-step process for conducting informational interviews:

Step 1. *Decide what you want to learn.* Are you researching a new career, a different industry, or both? Do you want advice about breaking into a field or about transferring your skills to a different line of work? Write down specifically what it is that you want to know.

Step 2. *Find people to interview.* Your family members, former co-workers, teachers, and other personal contacts may be able to put you in touch with people who you can contact to request a meeting. Tell them specifically what you are looking for (e.g. "I want to talk to someone who can help me learn about Web development jobs"). One of my clients found an excellent contact through her hairdresser! Otherwise, you will need to do research to find the names of individuals.

Decide who to contact based on job title. Do not contact human resources personnel unless you are considering a career in HR. If, for example, you want to learn about software programming, you will look for people with the title of software developer, senior software engineer, etc. If you are exploring a writing career, you will look for people with the title of editor, reporter, or feature writer.

If you want a broader understanding of an entire career track, you should speak with individuals at the level of director or vice president.

You must make your request for an informational interview to a specific person, not a title such as "manager of customer service." There are several ways to get the names of individuals.

- Trade/professional association Web sites sometimes post a directory of their members, which is an excellent source of contacts. If the organization produces a conference, the agenda will list speakers along with their title and company. Members of the association's management team may be able to suggest people to contact (and can provide information about general industry trends).

- Chamber of Commerce Web sites often list member organizations. This is a way to identify local companies within your area of interest.

- The online business networking site LinkedIn (www.linkedin.com) is another source of contacts. You can search by company name and see a list of employees who have LinkedIn profiles. If you find someone whose title matches your criteria, you can contact that individual about an informational interview. *(For best results, use postal mail to make your request. While you can create a profile and search on LinkedIn for free, you must pay for an upgraded account to email people that you are not connected with on the site. Most individuals will not respond to LinkedIn "Inmail" from people they don't know.)*

- Company Web sites sometimes include the names of employees in various departments.

Step 3. *Request an informational interview.* Once you have contact names, the next step is to send each person a letter or email to ask for a meeting. A written request is preferable to making a telephone call for several reasons. First, it eliminates the anxiety of calling someone you don't know and explaining who you are and what you want. Second, it gives the person you contact a chance to learn more about your background before you call them to set up a meeting. Third, a written communication shows that you are respectful that the person would take time from their busy schedule to help someone they have never met.

Keep a list or spreadsheet of everyone you contact, including the person's title, company, address, telephone number, email, and how you found him or her. This information is important for follow-up calls.

There are three elements to a query letter. The first is the opening, where you explain why you are contacting the individual. If you were referred by a mutual acquaintance, say so. Otherwise, explain how you got the person's name.

The second element is a brief summary of your work experience or education. This helps the person understand how they might assist you. The content of a discussion will be different if you are a recent graduate, for example, than if you have many years of work experience.

The third element is the request. You should let the individual know that you will be calling him or her within the next week to see whether you can meet. Include your telephone number, in case the person wants to contact you first.

You may also include a resume with your query letter so that the person learns more about your work history and skills. Remember that many people will not open email attachments from individuals they don't know. You will get better results if you send a letter and resume via postal mail.

The query letter should be brief (not more than one page). Here are two sample query letters. The first is to someone who was referred to you by a mutual acquaintance. The second is to someone whose name you found on your own.

Sample query letter to a mutual acquaintance

March 10, 2010

Mr. Michael Smith, Marketing Director
ACME Company
111 Corporate Drive
Anytown, USA 11111

Dear Mr. Smith:

My name is John Jones and I am interested in learning about career opportunities in product marketing. Paul Johnston [this is the name of the mutual acquaintance] thinks that you can give me some advice about how to break into the field.

For the past 3 years, I've worked in the product development department of Widget Works Computers. The work is interesting, however I am eager to use my creative skills to sell products rather than build them. The telecommunications industry has long been of interest to me, and I wonder how I could transfer my skills into that area. My resume is enclosed to give you an idea of my background.

I would like to meet with you to learn more about product marketing in telecommunications. I hope you won't mind a call next week to set up a time. If it's more convenient you can reach me at (555) 555-5555.

Sincerely,

John Jones
200 Maple Street
Anytown, USA 11111

Sample query letter to an individual you located on your own

September 3, 2010

Ms. Jane Smith, Editor
ACME Publishing Company
111 Corporate Drive
Anytown, USA 11111

Dear Ms. Smith:

My name is Sarah Jones and I am interested in learning about career opportunities in the children's book publishing field. I noticed that you are speaking on the topic of inspiring children's fiction at the National Children's Publishing Conference. I am eager to get your advice about how to break into the industry.

In May, I graduated from the Journalism Academy with a bachelor's degree in English. This summer, I completed a certificate program in children's literature from the Association for Quality in Youth Literature. My ultimate goal is to edit manuscripts for a major publisher, and I want to speak with you about where to begin my career.

I would like to meet with you to learn more about editorial careers in the children's publishing field. I hope you won't mind a call next week to see when we could get together. If it's more convenient you can reach me at (555) 555-5555.

Sincerely,

Jane Smith
200 Maple Street
Anytown, USA 11111

Step 4. *Follow up with a telephone call.* You will greatly increase your odds of getting a meeting if you follow up your letter or email with a telephone call. Keep your message brief. Identify yourself and remind the person why you are contacting him or her. Three or four sentences are usually sufficient. If you are nervous about making calls, write out a script and practice it until you feel confident (but don't practice so much that you sound like a machine!).

If you get voice mail, <u>leave a message</u>. If possible suggest one or two times that the person can call back and reach you. The times should be during regular business hours (e.g. "You can reach me between 10:00 and 11:30 tomorrow morning or Wednesday after 3:00pm"). If you don't receive a reply after three or four days, call again or send an email.

If after three attempts you do not get a response, presume that the individual cannot meet with you and do not continue making contact. Don't be discouraged if this happens. Not everyone you contact will say "yes."

SAMPLE TELEPHONE FOLLOW-UP SCRIPT FOR VOICE MAIL

"Hello, (state the person's name), this is John Jones. I'm calling to follow up on a letter I sent you last week. I'm exploring a career in product marketing, and Paul Johnston suggested that I contact you for some advice. I'm wondering if we can meet within the next week or two. You can reach me at (555) 555-5555 anytime after 11:00am. Thank you."

Step 5. *Prepare for your meeting as if it was a job interview.* Find out some information about the individual you will be meeting with and his or her company. The organization's Web site might include biographies of key employees. You can also search online networking sites, such as LinkedIn. This kind of preparation demonstrates that you take the informational interview seriously. It also gives you some talking points. For instance, you might discover that you and the individual share the same alma mater, once worked for the same company, or have a common interest.

Write down and practice speaking the questions that you plan to ask. Pay careful attention to your grooming and wear clothing is professional, clean and pressed. Bring a copy of your resume in case the individual asks to see it, or requests a copy to pass on to other people in the organization or his contact list. Arrive on time and greet the person you are meeting with in a polished manner—establish eye contact, smile, shake hands, and introduce yourself ("Hello, I'm John Jones, it's nice to meet you").

Here are some examples of questions to ask at an informational interview. You may have additional ones as well.

- How did you get into this field?
- What kind of education/experience is needed for this work?
- What does it take to be successful in this job/career/organization/industry?
- What surprised you about this job/career/organization/industry?
- How did you advance in your career?
- What are the employment prospects for someone entering this field?
- Which industry associations are you active in?
- What is a typical day like in your job?
- How much interaction do you have with others?
- Who else should I contact? May I use your name?

Do not ask the individual if there are any job openings at the company! The purpose of the meeting is for you to gather information. If you ask about a job, it will look like you arranged the discussion under false pretenses.

Respect the individual's time. Plan on a half-hour meeting and on asking six to seven questions. If the discussion is going well and you are uncertain about how much time has passed, ask whether the person has time for one or two more questions. When you leave thank the person for their time and ask for a business card.

Step 6. *Formally thank the person you met with.* Update your contact list or spreadsheet with notes about what happened at your meeting. Don't skip this step. You may want to renew contact with this individual in the future.

Always send a letter or email to formally thank the individual. This should be done within 48 hours of your meeting. Refer to one or two things that you spoke about, for example, "Thank you for giving me the Web site of the regional association chapter. I'll plan on attending their next meeting;" "I will contact John Jones, Sarah Smith and Beth Lewis this week and let you know what happens;" "I will look into the certification program that you mentioned."

 NT TIP: Update your contacts on what happens as a result of the information they give you. For example, "Thank you for recommending Ann Johnson to me. We met yesterday and she invited me to be her guest at the next meeting of the Direct Marketers Association." This will make a positive impression and is a way to begin developing networking contacts.

Assess Why You Are Not Getting Hired

"Whenever I am job hunting, I still have trouble understanding what the employer is looking for in a new employee."

Data Processor, age 46

Alex had been on more than 40 job interviews without receiving any call-backs or offers. Sean managed to get only one interview during the 18 months since he had graduated from college. Elizabeth was about ready to give up looking for work after sending out dozens of resumes without any response from employers.

These individuals, like so many job seekers I work with, had valuable skills to offer. Yet, after many long months of searching, they were getting nowhere. If you are having similar difficulties, this is the time to make an honest assessment of your situation and see what may be blocking you from gainful employment.

1. Seeking work in a highly competitive field. There are certain industries that attract many more qualified candidates than there are job openings (the performing arts, law, television, etc.). Other fields are so specialized that there are a very limited number of opportunities (astronomy, museum management, etc.). Changes in the economy, the introduction of a new technology, or a regulatory change can make some jobs scarce or obsolete. Career opportunities may also be limited by your geographic region. There will be many more chances for a broadcasting career in New York City, for example, than in rural Ohio.

The decision to enter into a very competitive field is a personal one. There are individuals who are willing to endure a protracted search for the chance to land a particular job. They may take "survival jobs" in the meantime in order to pay their bills. However, if becoming employed is your primary goal, you may need to choose a career in a field that is growing and that is in need of workers.

2. Lack of necessary skills. If you are responding to many job openings and not getting interviews, it may be that you do not have the required skills or experience. Alex realized, for example, that in order to get a job in the commercial graphic arts field, he had to learn HTML coding.

Most job postings include a mix of desired and required competencies. The candidates who are invited for interviews don't necessarily meet 100% of the listed criteria, but they possess the critical ones.

Critical skills are usually indicated with phrases like: "extensive/verifiable experience required in …;" "must include;" and "do not apply unless you meet these requirements." Negotiable skills are described with phrases like: "the ideal candidate will have;" "xyz experience preferred/desired;" "is a plus;" and "should be familiar with." Tasks and responsibilities are listed in descending order of importance, with the most important ones appearing first.

Do not take stated requirements too literally. I have had clients assume that they were not qualified for a job because they had 18 months of experience and the job posting asked for two years. Employers request the ideal and will relax requirements for candidates who possess key skills. Generally entry-level jobs are those that require up to two years experience; manager-level jobs require three to five years experience; director-level jobs five to ten years of experience; and senior-level positions ten-plus years of relevant experience.

You should not disqualify yourself if a job requires "good teamwork/people skills" and the "ability to multitask." People skills and multitasking can mean very different things depending on the specific job, the industry, or a particular company. People skills will be much more important in jobs where you are dealing directly with customers,

---

DETERMINE YOUR QUALIFICATIONS WITH A DISCREPANCY ANALYSIS

A discrepancy analysis is a useful tool when you are unsure about whether you are qualified for a particular kind of work. Print four to six ads for the position you want. On a sheet of paper, write down the specific skills, experience and educational requirements mentioned in each ad. Write negotiable items (those described as "a plus," "desired," etc.) in a separate section. Then, circle all of the items that match your background. If there is a requirement for a four-year degree and you have one, circle that item. If you have experience using a specified piece of machinery or software program, circle that, too.

The items that are not circled show the discrepancy between your skills the employer's requirements. Sometimes, the discrepancy is minor and not an impediment to employment, like a few months difference between your length of experience and what is requested in the ad. If you are missing significant skills, you need to acquire them first before looking for work.

It is at this point that some people get discouraged and want to abandon an occupation. "I can't afford to go back to school and get another degree," they say. Many are surprised to learn that they can acquire skills without getting a formal degree. Certificate or other training programs can provide needed skills in a few months. You might also find related careers with less stringent educational requirements or for which you are already qualified.

managing staff, or working with people in different departments of the organization. Face-to-face interaction will be more complicated than contact via telephone or the Internet. Multitasking at a three-person law firm will probably be more manageable than multitasking in the marketing department of a major software company.

3. Unrealistic expectations. Some individuals remain unemployed because their expectations about what it takes to be considered for the job or what they are qualified to do does not match with reality. Examples of unrealistic expectations include: being hired for a management role when you have no work experience; insisting that every single aspect of a job fits your ideal; requesting a salary that is too high; finding work in a specialized industry where you have no experience.

4. Not spending enough time on the job search. Finding a job is hard work and requires consistent effort over time. One man, with very good qualifications, came to see me perplexed about why he hadn't landed an interview after nearly six months. It turns out that he was spending between one to three hours *per week* on his job search—hardly enough time to be successful! It is imperative that you develop a realistic search plan. Set aside time every day to make phone calls, send out resumes and thank you letters, arrange informational interviews and do more research.

5. Responding only to posted job openings. The majority of my coaching clients rely on this single strategy to find work. The problem is that only 5% of people find their jobs through help wanted ads. According to the U.S. Department of Labor Statistics, 48% of people find jobs through networking; 24% via direct contact with an employer; and 23% through employment and other agencies. You will increase your chances of getting work multiple times by including three to five different strategies in your search.

Job search strategies include: networking … posting a resume on Internet job boards … contacting a recruiter/employment agency … strategic volunteering to gain experience and make contacts in your desired field … joining a professional association … working at internships or temporary jobs … attending career fairs.

6. Ineffective resume. The purpose of a resume is to present your skills, experience and accomplishments relevant to the job that you are seeking *now*. It should not be a review of every single task that you performed at every job that you have ever held. An employer is unlikely to read through a long resume that is packed with irrelevant details. Many resumes are screened by computers need to include the key words and phrases that match the job to which you are applying. There are some individuals who do not provide enough information about their qualifications. Peter, for example, worked at a historical association for three years, yet listed his experience simply as "Researcher." After reviewing his job duties, we expanded his description to say, "Conducted primary research using journal databases, monographs, library materials, and the Internet."

Be definitive when you describe your skills and abilities. Avoid qualifiers like "some experience using spreadsheets," or "moderate computer skills."

In most cases, your resume should be one or two pages long and list jobs that you've held within the past decade. If your relevant job experience goes back farther than ten years, consider consolidating some positions under a single heading. For example, Jill listed three jobs under the category of "Early Writing Experience" and summarized her primary tasks in two sentences. If you are looking for work in two or three different fields, create different versions of your resume to highlight your most relevant experience in each.

If you are changing careers, structure your resume so that pertinent skills, experience and training are presented first. Jack retrained as a paralegal after being fired from several engineering jobs. In between the last engineering position and his paralegal training, he spent three years working at a retail store. Jack's original resume was a hodgepodge that began with details about his retail duties. It also included every job that he had held since high school, and a long section describing his advanced engineering degree. His paralegal training and experience were mentioned last.

Together we re-worked his resume so that his paralegal studies and 4.0 GPA are listed first, followed by his twelve months of experience at a local law firm. His engineering career is summarized in a single paragraph. The retail experience is de-emphasized and Jack is ready to explain his years at the store.

The pragmatic nature of many people with Asperger's Syndrome can result in resumes that list lots of job tasks but few or no accomplishments. Whenever possible, include examples of how you saved money, improved efficiency, increased sales or revenue or otherwise made an outstanding contribution (e.g. achievement awards). These examples illustrate the difference between tasks and accomplishments:

Task	*Accomplishment*
Operated cash register…	*Accurately handled an average of 35 transactions per hour*
Marketing copywriting…	*Created direct marketing promotions that generated a 3% response rate*
Wrote articles…	*Interviewed industry leaders for articles about efficient data center management published in DataDecisions magazine*

Proofread your resume and cover letter carefully! They are the first impression an employer has of you. Inconsistent formatting, typographical errors and spelling mistakes will land your resume in the "no" pile. One of my clients seeking a copy editing job emphasized his attention to detail … yet had three typos on his resume! Your email address must also be professional. Would you want to hire loafer@xyz.com?

7. Looking in too many different job categories. For best results, limit your search to no more than three different kinds of jobs. Otherwise, you will not be able to make the number of contacts necessary for results. If you are not sure what kind of work you are qualified for, seek guidance from a coach, career counselor or from your state employment office. Sending out dozens of resumes for positions that you are not qualified for wastes your time and the employer's.

8. Ineffective interviewing skills. It is imperative that you are able to communicate your qualifications at job interviews. There are many books and Web sites that offer excellent advice about interviewing. If you are confused about how to apply the information to your situation, find a professional who can help you with interviewing skills.

Tips for Job Interviews

The person who interviews you for a job wants to determine whether your skills, talents and experience match the requirements of an open position. It is important that you understand the purpose of common interview questions so that you can provide the information that the interviewer wants. If you take questions too literally or out of context he or she will get confused. For example, Derrick was flummoxed when he was asked, "So, why should I hire you instead of the other candidates?" After thinking about it for a few seconds, he replied, "I don't know how to answer that question, because I haven't met the other candidates." The interviewer was aware that Derrick had not met the other people who had interviewed for the position. He was asking that Derrick summarize why he believed that he was the person who should be hired.

A hiring manager concluded her interview with Jack by remarking, "Don't hesitate to ask if you have any additional questions." As Jack reached the elevator, he realized that he did have another question and promptly returned to the manager's office to ask it. When he returned a second time with a question, she asked him to leave. The hiring manager expected that if Jack had additional questions, he would either call or email her after he returned home.

When I work with clients on their interviewing skills, we do mock interviews. I assume the role of the interviewer and ask questions which the client has already been practicing how to answer. I record my reaction to the client's replies, and then we talk about what went well and where improvement is needed.

I have developed guidelines in response to questions that my clients frequently ask about interviewing:

- When you meet the interviewer, remember to smile, make eye contact and shake hands.
- Introduce yourself, even though the interviewer knows who you are because you have an appointment.
- Smiling is important when you are introduced, to convey friendliness, and at select points during the interview to convey enthusiasm.
- If you arrive more than 15 minutes early, find a place to get a cup of coffee. If you don't drink coffee, find someplace else to wait until it is ten minutes before your scheduled appointment.
- Prepare some small talk in advance so that you have something to say during the dreaded walk to the interviewer's office. Staring straight ahead without saying a word makes a bad impression.
- If the interviewer doesn't tell you where to sit, don't stand there waiting for instructions. Select a chair near the person's desk and be seated.
- Even though your resume describes your work experience, the interviewer expects you to elaborate on your previous jobs.
- "Tell me about yourself" means "summarize your relevant work experience."
- Don't speak in a monotone or stare at the floor or ceiling.
- When asked about why you want to work at the company, don't say, "Because you have an opening."
- If the interview is over in ten minutes or less, you probably will not be called back.
- At the end of the interview, express your interest in the job, even if you are not sure if you really want to work there.
- If you remember a question when you are at the elevator, go home and send an email.

CHAPTER THREE

Communication Skills at Work

> *"One reason I was successful as a Peace Corps volunteer is because they train everyone on how to act in the foreign culture. If I could have lessons on how to act in the U.S. it wouldn't be so bad for me here."*
>
> *IT Specialist, age 47*

I believe that problems with interpersonal communication account for 85% of the difficulties that those individuals with Asperger's Syndrome face in the workplace. After all, neurotypicals are a socially oriented lot. Most correlate their satisfaction at work directly to the quality of their relationships with supervisors and co-workers. The "social stuff" even plays a role in who is hired and who is fired. Several times during my corporate career I was involved in decisions about layoffs. Usually, choices were made based on who got along better with other people.

Learning "good enough" communication skills is, in my opinion, the most important thing that you can do for your career. Too often, the communication problems of people with Asperger's Syndrome are treated like attitude or behavior problems. This is not because NTs are insensitive or mean. It is because neurotypicals and Aspergians process information differently.

In contrast to the "we" orientation of neurotypicals, Aspergians have more of a "me" orientation. If you are a typical person with AS, you have a hard time identifying the desires, expectations, motives and needs of others, unless they are explicitly stated. You respond to situations based on your point of view, presuming that others understand and agree with it. As one of my clients explained, "I have little or no accurate sense for what would be appropriate to any other given person, or to any situation that involves anyone other than me."

Neurotypicals base much of their interpersonal communication on their intuitive grasp of "The Big Picture." They are quickly able to integrate information from their senses, memory and emotions to size up a situation and decide on a response. If a staff member makes a mistake, the NT manager will consider the severity of the error, context in which it occurred, and the work history of the individual before deciding what to do. Thus, a manager might decide to overlook a minor typo made by an employee with an excellent track record ... especially if the manager knows that the person was working under a tight deadline. Unlike NTs, Aspergians focus on details, piecing together discrete facts until the big picture emerges. This can be a laborious and time consuming process and the big picture may get lost along the way. A person with Asperger's Syndrome considers a mistake to be a mistake and does not hesitate to point it out.

Emotions also play a role in neurotypical communications. An NT will anticipate how someone is or will feel about an event. This requires knowledge of some of the other person's characteristics. For instance, if I know that recognition is important to Paula, I may decide to thank her publicly for her work on a special project; perhaps at the next department meeting. If I know that Steve is anxious about speaking in front of a group, I ask him to make a brief remark and work with him on his public speaking skills.

Scripts, as you probably already know, are of limited value in the "real world." It is impossible to anticipate and draft responses for every interaction that could happen in single day (never mind over the course of one's career!). Scripts can be of value for explaining unexpected behaviors, making requests and for initiating basic conversation. However, they are not sufficient for dealing with the complexity of human interaction in the workplace.

So what is "good enough" communication? I define it as the ability to interact with others in a manner that is perceived as professional and personable. Good enough communication means that you understand what is expected of you, know how to clarify anything that is not clear, and are able to work with others in a group. It does not require that you become a phony or lie.

As you read through the communication techniques in this chapter, remember that in the typical workplace, people are hired based on their skills, experience and ability to "fit in." If you violate cultural norms, you will alienate your colleagues. People do not want to work with individuals who make them feel uncomfortable.

Pragmatics, Central Coherence and Theory of Mind at Work

"Mental exhaustion comes from having to figure things out cognitively rather than intuitively. If I seem 'slow,' it is because I have to deliberately think things through."

Web Content Administrator, age 42

Sean had tried for months to land an entry-level IT position. He was excited about the prospect of working at a small software firm. After successful interviews with the human resources manager and his potential supervisor, Sean returned to meet with two members of the IT department.

Sean listened as they described their roles at the company, and then commented that their jobs sounded very simple. He was surprised when he received a phone call from the human resources manager telling him that his arrogance had cost him the job. "I figured that by telling them that their jobs were simple, they would see how smart I am and want to hire me."

Kevin's supervisor asked him to take a look at some new scheduling software that the company had recently purchased. Two weeks later, the supervisor confronted Kevin, angrily inquiring why he wasn't using the software. "I *did* take a look at it," Kevin explained to him, "but I didn't think it would be useful so I deleted it off my computer. If my boss wanted me to use it, why didn't he just say so?"

If you have experienced similar kinds of miscommunication, each incident probably leaves you more confused, frustrated and anxious. By understanding the differences in how Aspergians and neurotypicals process information, it will be easier to develop strategies for interacting effectively on the job. The processing differences involve pragmatics, central coherence and theory of mind.

Spoken words account for about 7% of human communication. Most of the meaning of what we say is derived from how words are spoken (volume and tone of voice, inflection, rate of speech) and non-verbally via body language (facial expression, eye contact, position of one's body, proximity to others, etc.). In Kevin's case, he focused only the supervisor's words: "I want you to take a look at the software." He missed the real (inferred) meaning of what was said: "I want you look at the new software program and start using it." This is an example of pragmatics, which is the use of language within a social context.

Context is what enables people to adjust their communication to fit a particular situation. Within the context of business etiquette, a person knows to speak more formally to a member of the senior management team than to a co-worker. Within the context of a business meeting, an individual will adjust the content of a presentation depending upon the audience. When talking with a customer, the context of the business relationship dictates focusing on addressing the needs of the client.

Central coherence refers to awareness of the big picture, which is also known as "getting the gist" of a situation. Although it is often discussed in relation to executive functions, it also plays a role in communication. In order to figure out the right thing to say, a person needs an understanding of the overall situation. Then, he can focus on all of the pertinent information and ignore irrelevant details. "There are many times when I have made an assessment of a situation and then made a decision," said Aaron, "only to find that I missed something major."

This is how central coherence works. You plan to ask you plan to ask your boss for a raise. On Monday morning you see her in the hallway. You notice that her hair is styled differently than usual and that she is wearing high heeled shoes instead of her usual flats. Her large gold necklace catches your attention and you wonder if she bought it as a set with the matching earrings. As you walk toward her, you repeat in your mind again and again how you will request a meeting. You silently count out the pattern in the carpet: three light blue squares followed by a large dark blue stripe. As you make your way down the hallway, you notice out of the corner of your eye that all of the offices are empty. The clock on the wall says 8:53am. You finally reach your supervisor and ask to meet. To your surprise, she replies (in an annoyed tone of voice), "Can't you see that this is not a good time?!"

Although you noticed many details about the environment, your supervisor's reaction indicates that you missed something important.

Let's take another look at your boss in that hallway. When you see her you also notice that she glances at her watch and take quick steps in the direction of the conference room, indicating that she is in a hurry. You hear the sound of distant chattering while simultaneously passing empty offices. You realize that the vice presidents have assembled in the conference room and are waiting for a meeting to begin. The smell of eggs, bacon and coffee reminds you that whenever the senior management team convenes, they are served a catered breakfast. You recall that your boss spent most of the previous Thursday and Friday working on a presentation.

This time, you noticed the pieces of information which suggested that your boss is running late for an important meeting ... and that this is definitely not the time to approach her about a raise! Details which were irrelevant to the situation at hand were filtered out of your consciousness, such as the pattern in the rug, the exact time, and your boss's gold jewelry. Important details, such as your supervisor's rushed appearance, the sounds coming from the conference room, and the empty offices of the vice presidents were not. This is an example of strong central coherence in action.

For many people with Asperger's Syndrome, the drive for central coherence is not as strong as it is for neurotypicals. Sometimes, like in Aaron's case, important pieces of information get lost within the minutia, and the big picture is obscured.

Theory of mind, or awareness of another person's point of view, is a third component of communication. This is the ability to recognize that other people have thoughts, desires, knowledge and motives that differ from yours. Theory of mind is what allows you to make educated guesses about how someone will respond to a situation, what they are feeling or what they would like you to do.

Individuals vary in their theory of mind abilities. The weaker a person's theory of mind, the more random and confusing the actions of other people will seem. Alice, for example, could not reconcile that her supervisor praised her outstanding programming skill, while also insisting that Alice release products with code that was not perfect. "Why won't he let me do good work?" she fumed. "It's a lie for the company to say that the products are top quality."

Alice's supervisor, however, was responsible for making sure that products were available for sale in time to meet quarterly revenue targets and market demands. From his perspective, the company's products are top quality because they out sell competing brands and earn high ratings in the trade press and from customers. The supervisor is also aware that customers expect a certain number of imperfections in any piece of software. Alice's weak theory of mind skills prevented her from considering her supervisor's point of view, and, as a result, his decisions didn't make sense to her.

Pragmatics, the drive for central coherence and theory of mind all played a role in Sandra's dilemma. As production manager for a small specialty publishing company, Sandra formats editorial copy, positions advertisements, and works with a printer to assure the timely delivery of magazines to the mail house. At her last performance review, Sandra was praised for her meticulous attention to detail and perfect on-time production record.

One Monday afternoon, David, the managing editor, informed Sandra that the feature article for the company's flagship publication would be late. It was being rewritten to include some breaking industry news. Sandra would not receive copy for the article as expected on Tuesday morning. In fact, David wasn't exactly sure when she would get the final manuscript, "but it will definitely be by the end of the week."

This meant that Sandra would not have time to get a final layout to Ed, the editor-in-chief, on Friday morning. "David knows the deadlines and that Ed always signs off on a final layout," Sandra exclaimed. "When

I asked David if he wanted to review the production schedule, he said no, and that the rewrites were in the best interest of the readers. He told me I had to be flexible and figure out how to make up the lost time. How is sending the magazine out late in the best interest of readers?!"

By focusing exclusively on production deadlines, Sandra missed the bigger picture, which was the importance of incorporating breaking news into the magazine's feature article. She didn't look at the situation from David's perspective. His job was to ensure a quality editorial product and breaking news took precedence over meeting production deadlines.

To Sandra, David's comments about being flexible were puzzling. "What option do I have but to miss the deadline? The situation is pretty black and white: David didn't care about deadlines; the magazine will be late; and I will be blamed because other people are not following the rules."

To get a broader picture of the situation, Sandra and I analyzed it in the following way:
- Separate facts from emotional reactions to the situation
- Explore the reason that something is happening; does it make sense?
- Review her previous on-the-job experiences
- Brainstorm options

When Sandra initially heard that the copy would be late, she became overwhelmed about missing a deadline. She spent nearly 20 minutes crying in her office. When we looked at the facts, the situation was less daunting. Breaking news, on a topic of interest to readers, conflicted with the magazine's usual production deadlines. David decided that readers would value his commentary on the news, and that they wouldn't be upset if the magazine arrived a few days late. "It makes sense that David wants to rewrite the article," Sandra said.

She then thought back to a previous job that she had at a newspaper. "Stories were late all the time," she said, "My boss used to build extra days into the production schedule because of it." Then she smiled, "I can do the same thing!"

We also brainstormed other options that Sandra had to deal with the late article. One was to call the printer to see if the magazine could be produced more quickly. She called, the answer was yes, and the issue arrived only two days late.

Once she analyzed the situation, David's decision made sense. His focus on the bigger picture led him to assume that Sandra would understand his reasoning for why the article would be late. He expected her to be proactive in revising the production schedule.

Increasing your theory of mind skills and awareness of situational context requires the you become a good detective. In addition to observing clues in a person's body language (which is discussed later in this chapter), you can learn a lot through the use of the "who, what where, why, how" questions. Advance planning, when possible, can also make interpersonal communication easier. Here is an example of how it works.

Andy was excited to start his new accounting job, but nervous about the "welcome aboard" lunch that was scheduled to take place on his first day. The luncheon was going to include four of Andy's fellow new hires, Andy's supervisor, and the head of the department. Despite his extroversion and desire to fit in, communication didn't come easily to Andy. "I don't want to do anything dumb on my first day!" he said.

We began by clarifying the purpose of the lunch. Andy was surprised when I explained that it was a chance for people to get to know each other, and that the conversation would not focus strictly on accounting. Andy's special interest was numbers. During stressful events, such as this gathering with people he doesn't know, Andy would look for opportunities to turn the conversation to the merits of various tax deductions, the toughest questions on the CPA exam, or his projected 401k savings at retirement.

We then went through a series of "who, what, where, why, how" questions like these, that he could use to prepare for the lunch and other situations:

- Who will be attending? What are their concerns, needs and purpose for being there? What is their rank in the organization (e.g. members of your department, senior management team, etc.)?

- What is the reason for the meeting? Is it a routine gathering of department members to update each other on project status? A company-wide announcement from the CEO? Are you discussing a contract with a customer or vendor, or meeting with your boss for a performance review? Or is it a social event such as a holiday celebration or birthday luncheon?

- Where is the meeting being held? In the boardroom (which suggests a formal discussion) or at the park for this year's summer outing?

- What does the other person or group members know about the topic? If they have little or no prior knowledge, you will have to prepare a detailed explanation. If they are very familiar with the topic, then a summary is in order.

Knowing that Andy would have to engage in small talk for the purpose of establishing good relationships with his co-workers, we practiced questions that he could ask, and how he could enter into conversations and keep them going. (Small talk is discussed later in this chapter.) Since most of the people attending the lunch didn't know each other, we anticipated that each individual might be asked to introduce him or herself and give a brief summary of their background. We also anticipated that the meal would be at a sit-down restaurant, but not the fanciest one in town. Thus Andy would dress as he usually did for the office.

The analysis and process of going through the questions on this list can be mentally exhausting. Some of my clients complain that it isn't possible to go through a series of such questions for every situation. They are right. However, analysis makes it possible to create templates for events that are likely to occur again. It also provides a way to handle impromptu situations so that you become better at communicating. It takes time and practice, but it does get easier.

Making the Right First Impression

Every job requires some form of communication with other people. Even if you are self-employed, you are interacting with customers, vendors, and other service providers, such as a bookkeeper. Most of these individuals will be NTs. The expression that you only get one chance to make a first impression is true. Research has shown that most people begin forming opinions about others within the first 30 seconds of meeting. Once an opinion is formed, it is usually hard to change.

The impression you make during the first days and weeks in a new job will be lasting. In addition to being evaluated on your ability to perform the job, you are being evaluated on whether you "fit in" to the organization. All companies hire employees on a conditional basis, whether stated or not. This probationary status can last from two weeks to three months.

There are several things that you can do to make a positive first impression on your colleagues.

• *Treat the first days and weeks on the job as a time to learn about specific job tasks, your co-workers and how things get done at this company.* Do not suggest different ways to do things until you understand how and why tasks are done in the current manner. Certain procedures probably affect other areas of the company in ways that you are not aware.

• *Listen and follow instructions.* Do not insist on doing things your own way; this will irritate your supervisor and co-workers. Stay within your assigned areas of responsibility. It is not okay to start doing someone else's work, even if you believe that you can do it better, or to begin your own project because you are bored. If you finish your assigned tasks early, ask your supervisor what you should do next.

• *Arrive on time, neatly dressed and properly groomed.* Your appearance is a form of non-verbal communication. If you look sloppy, people may assume that your work is sloppy, too. Whether you wear a uniform or clothing of your own choosing, make sure that what you wear is clean, neat and pressed and complies with the company's dress code. You want co-workers to focus on your abilities, not your wrinkled clothes, unusual hairstyle or body odor!

• *Refrain from making negative comments about your current or previous supervisors, co-workers or employers.* Your new co-workers want to work with people who are pleasant and enthusiastic. They avoid people who are perceived as chronic complainers. We all encounter frustrations on the job and need to vent these frustrations to others. Until you know who you can trust to keep your communication private, make only positive comments at work.

• *Wait until people finish speaking before you begin talking.* Interrupting people makes them think that you are not listening or not interested in what they have to say. One man, who works from a home office, keeps his phone on "mute" during meetings as a reminder to let people finish speaking before he makes a comment. If you are concerned that you will forget your point if you don't speak up right away, make notes. Some people carry a note pad for this purpose.

Another technique is to have a co-worker who you trust give you subtle signals when you interrupt. You can arrange this by saying, "I want to break my habit of interrupting. Would you [cough, clear your throat, tap you ear, etc.] to let me know when I do it?"

• *Practice active listening.* These are things to do to show that you are paying attention and understand what a speaker is trying to communicate. Active listening skills include: making an appropriate amount of eye contact; nodding you head in agreement periodically; and making brief comments such as, "I see," "I understand" from time to time. Observe people engaged in conversation and you will notice them engaged in active listening.

 NT TIP: It will make a poor impression to have potentially offensive or controversial items on display in your cubicle or office. This includes photographs that are graphic or sexually-oriented, political material, etc. The goal is to fit in, not to stand out.

Communicating with Body Language

Even though they are often not consciously aware of it, NTs use body language to communicate information about what they are thinking and feeling. Body language, along with vocal intonation, is a form of non-verbal communication. Body language includes facial expressions, posture, gestures (especially of the arms and hands), and your physical proximity to others.

Body language can communicate basic emotions, such as happiness, sadness, anger or fear. It can also provide data about others that can help you understand situations at work that will not be obvious based on someone's words alone.

After ten weeks, Tom's customer service supervisor was not happy with his performance. Tom had disclosed having Asperger's Syndrome a month earlier. I had met with Tom, his supervisor, Nancy, and the human resources manager to discuss Tom's accommodations and performance short falls. Now Tom, Nancy and I were meeting again to review Tom's progress.

My first hint that Nancy was not filled with great expectations about Tom's ability to do the job came when she entered the reception area and nodded a hello, deftly avoiding my handshake. When we reached the conference room, Tom was already seated. I listened as Nancy dutifully reviewed each item in his performance improvement plan. Her voice was tense and her eyes were fixed on the form in front of her. She gazed briefly at Tom as she delivered clipped answers to his questions and rhythmically tapped her pen against her palm. At the end of the meeting, I inquired about how long Tom had to make the required improvements. "Immediately," Nancy replied, looking me straight in the eye. I winced inside.

Nancy's refusal to shake my hand and her silence as we walked from the reception area to the conference room told me immediately that she was not happy to be having the meeting. Otherwise, she would have followed the standard NT protocol of eye contact, a smile, handshake and small talk. The tension in her voice, brief glances at Tom and continual pen tapping signaled her impatience. "She's going through the motions," I thought. An engaged NT would have looked Tom in the eye and spoken in a friendly, earnest tone. Very likely, gestures, such as a nod of the head or the folding of one's hands in front of the body, would have been used to communicate attention and concern. In choosing to punctuate the word "immediately" with a stare, Nancy made it very clear to me that she had run out of patience with Tom.

After the meeting, Tom and I went to the employee cafeteria to talk about what happened. "I think that went pretty well," Tom said. I told him that I didn't agree. I described to Tom my impression of the conversation, and we reviewed what he could do to try and meet Nancy's expectations. Unfortunately, he was let go a week and a half later. It turned out that the meeting was a formality and the decision had already been made.

Observing body language can help gauge another person's level of confidence, enthusiasm, nervousness, excitement, boredom, and other states of mind. You can also deduce what someone wants you to do, such as a join them in a conversation or activity, not interrupt a meeting they are having with someone else, come back later, stop talking, leave, etc.

People also use body language to signal what they want to do, such as get back to their work, change topics, end the meeting, etc.

 NT TIP: When an NT is ready to end a conversation or meeting, he or she often speaks in the past tense, as in, "It was nice to meet you;" "I'm glad we had the chance to get that settled;" "This was a good discussion." Nonverbal cues include closing an open file folder, pushing their chair back slightly, glancing at the computer screen, folding their arms, and standing up.

You can find many books that describe the meaning behind body language. There are books written for people on the autism spectrum, such as *The Social Skills Picture Book for High School and Beyond,* by Dr. Jed Baker. There are computerized tests that measure your ability to interpret facial expressions. At the urging of a client, I took an online test and found the examples difficult to decipher. My score was very low! A better option, in my opinion, is to watch movies or television programs with the sound turned down and try to deduce what the characters are thinking and feeling.

In addition to observing other people's body language, it is important that you pay attention to your own. Otherwise, you might be sending unintended messages to others. NTs will think that you are disinterested, bored, detached, angry or aloof if you:

- Stare at the floor or ceiling during a conversation
- Slump in your chair
- Fold your arms across your chest
- Fiddle with a pen, rubber band or paper clip during a conversation
- Speak in a monotone, too softly, too loudly or too quickly (tape record your voice and hear how your speech sounds to others)
- Stare into space as you try to think of an answer to a question (instead say, "Let me think about that for a moment")
- Stare at them (looking directly into their eyes for ten seconds or more)
- Don't smile (this conveys unfriendliness and makes NTs uneasy)

With practice, most people can improve their ability to recognize and interpret body language. If you find decoding body language very difficult or impossible, explain the situation using neutral language. By explaining that you are having difficulty, people will not take your behavior personally. For example: "I have trouble reading body language—can you tell me what you're thinking?"; "Sometimes when I'm concentrating, I forget to say hello. Please don't take it personally"; "People tell me that I look angry when I'm lost in thought. Tell me if you notice that."

Small Talk: Key to Relationship Building

"I didn't know that just saying, 'Hi, how are you?' is a key to opening relationships, not a question that needs answering."

Food Service Worker and Educator, age 56

Ah, small talk. That nonsensical NT ritual where people waste time talking about vapid subjects that no one really cares about.

You probably agree with the preceding statement. You probably also wonder on a regular basis why you should bother with something that is not only dumb, but hard to do.

Small talk is an important part of success at work because it is the first step in establishing relationships with your colleagues. Most NTs place a high value on workplace relationships. A good relationship with one's supervisor and liking one's co-workers are consistently rated as major factors for job satisfaction.

At the most superficial level, trading a few friendly remarks with fellow employees you see in the lunch room or in the elevator sends the message that you consider yourself part of the group. Sharing small talk with the people you work with on projects is the basis for building camaraderie and trust. NTs want to work with people who they like and who are dependable. They are usually much more forgiving of errors and eccentricities if they perceive you as cooperative and friendly.

You do need to actually like someone to act friendly toward them at work. These are things that you can do to make yourself likeable:

- Greet co-workers in the morning by saying "Good morning" or asking "Hi, how are you?"
- Smile when you greet people or pass them in the hallway. If necessary, practice this skill so that is becomes natural. A person who doesn't smile often comes across as angry, unfriendly or bored.
- Join your colleagues for lunch on a regular basis. Attend office holiday parties and talk to people while you are there, even if you only converse with people in your department. Act like you are having a good time, even if you are not.
- Show an interest in others, both in the projects they are working on and how they are personally.

NT TIP: Be gracious when someone gives you a compliment by smiling and saying thank you. It is considered rude to reject the compliment by explaining why you don't deserve it ("The work was easy and I had no trouble with it") or questioning the person's taste ("What do you find attractive about an old watch?").

How to Make a Reasonable Amount of Small Talk

The basic formula for small talk is the discussion of general, neutral topics for short periods of time, usually no more than 5 minutes. Neutral topics are the weather, traffic, sports, a national news item, or weekend plans. Topics to avoid are those that polarize people, such as politics, religion, or race; or topics that make people uncomfortable, such as sexual topics and gossip about other employees. Personal observations about a person's weight, clothing, hair style and mannerisms should also be avoided.

Despite being a talented software developer, Susan has been fired from numerous jobs. "I've been lambasted for being 'rude,' 'nasty,' and 'offensive' for saying things that I thought were benign or supportive," she complained. She was sharing lunch with a co-worker who was lamenting about numerous failed weight loss attempts. Intending to be sympathetic, Susan said, "I can see that the diets aren't working because you're still fat." The co-worker complained to Susan's supervisor and the comment, combined with other affronts, got Susan fired. Months later, she was still confused. "How could the co-worker be so insulted?" she asked, "I'm fat myself!"

You can find neutral topics for small talk, even if you do not follow sports teams or popular programs on television. Many local news stations have Web sites that summarize top stories. This is a quick way to stay informed about what is happening in your community so you will be able to contribute to discussions. You might become interested in these subjects.

The key to effective small talk is to keep the conversation going for at least two or three turns. The point is not to exchange information; it is to form connections with others. Some of these connections will remain superficial and others might become more substantive.

Do not respond to comments or questions with one-word answers or by saying "I don't know." That will be interpreted as your wanting to end the conversation. You are in the break room and someone asks whether you saw a particular program or sports event. You say, "No." You have sent a message that you do not want to interact with the individual. Instead, ask a question or make a comment to express your interest in the other person, such as, "I haven't seen that program, what is it about?" or "What is your favorite team?"

 NT TIP: A highly recommended resource for learning conversational skills is *How to Start a Conversation and Make Friends* by Don Gabor.

Another example of how small talk can be a bridge to establishing a relationship: someone asks, "Did you get caught in that traffic jam on Route 66?" Instead of saying "no," you say, "No, I live in Smithtown so I don't take the highway to get here." Other person responds, "I used to drive through Smithtown when I worked at ACME Widgetworks." You reply, "I worked at ACME six years ago in the R&D group." Your new acquaintance says, "I was in R&D, too. We should get together for lunch this week."

Small talk is what commonly leads to a new contact in your network, a buddy at work and sometimes a personal friendship. Even though it may feel very uncomfortable for you at first, it is an important business skill to learn. I work with my clients to find what I call "stealth" ways to practice small talk, such as striking up conversations with store clerks, bank tellers, and the mailman. Do not give up if your initial efforts aren't "perfect." It gets easier the more that you do it.

Another way to develop relationships at work is to become curious about the people you interact with on a regular basis. Select one or two individuals in your department or team whom you would like to know better. You can be curious about their career: how long they have been employed at this company, where they worked before, what their job involves (if you don't already know) or why they chose this career. You can also become curious about general personal information: what town the person lives in, whether they are married or have children and what their interests are outside of work.

As with small talk, it is important to keep a discussion going with questions and supporting comments about a topic. For instance, if you ask a colleague, "How long have you worked for this company?" and she answers, "Six years," and you reply, "Oh," the conversation will screech to a halt. But if you ask another, related question like, "Have you always worked in the marketing department?" the discussion will continue. You should be ready to answer some questions about yourself, too.

Building relationships at work takes time and consistent effort. You need to behave in ways that signal your willingness to connect. Sam realized that sitting at his cubicle with headphones on all day was seen by others as a message to "stay away." Bill "forced" himself to leave his office door open for several hours a day, so that he would be perceived as accessible by his colleagues.

It must be stressed that you do not need to be interacting with other people all of the time, or become a world-class communicator to fit in. The key is to do enough to establish yourself as open, friendly and trustworthy. If you make a sincere effort to have positive working relationships with others, people will very likely sense that and accept some awkwardness or social gaffes. They will also make an effort to have a positive working relationship with you.

Why You Need a Work Buddy

"Instead of trying to fit in with numerous people at once, find one who fits in well with the others and allow the person to instruct you as you go along. I have a co-worker who jokingly states that he will help, 'take the ass out of Asperger's.'"

Inventory Control Specialist, age 32

Many years ago, I read that someone had figured out 200 different ways to wash dishes. Their point was that there are many different methods for achieving the same result.

This is also true in the workplace. Every organization has unique systems, processes and procedures. For example, if you change jobs, you might discover that the new company uses different software programs, ordering systems, budgeting procedures, or status reports. Reporting structures may be different. Certainly the people will be, and they will have different expectations, preferences and communication styles. The company culture might also be a departure from your previous experience (see Chapter Four for A Primer on Office Politics).

The unique way that "things get done around here" can only be learned on the job, and from your co-workers. This is why I believe that one of the most important strategies you can implement is to find a "work buddy."

A work buddy is a colleague, preferably a peer or someone in your department. This should not be your supervisor or a human resources representative. This is someone who can help you to understand and learn the many specific details about how to do your job and interact with others in the company. Sometimes, this is a formally established partnership with a designated mentor or trainer. More often, a work buddy is someone who you like and trust.

There are many benefits of having a work buddy. He can translate unspoken workplace rules for you: what is a priority, how your supervisor prefers to get information, whom you can trust and whom you should avoid. He can explain office politics—who in the organization really has power, how decisions get made, what qualities are valued, and how various departments or divisions interact.

Your buddy can also provide concrete ideas about how to work efficiently. Paul, for example, was overwhelmed by the weekly volume of patients that he had to manage in his job as a physician assistant. He couldn't determine whether he was processing paperwork too slowly or simply had too many patients to see. Paul asked his buddy, a fellow physician assistant, to review his case-management methods. The co-worker showed Paul short cuts that saved four hours of administrative time per week.

Dan's buddy was able to give him excellent advice about how to handle various conflicts and frustrations. Once, he stopped Dan from sending an angry email to the director of the computing department. "He talked me out of something that could really have damaged my reputation," Dan said.

We all need a reality check from time to time, and this is another way that your work buddy can be of great value. This person can provide feedback about things such as: Is my supervisor critical of just my work, or of everyone else's, too? Are other people confused by the new system, or it is just me? Is everyone overwhelmed or am I the only one who can't keep up? Do other departments have conflicts with the head of marketing or is it only my group? Was that comment a joke or a put down?

Choose your work buddy with care. This person needs to be someone whom you explicitly trust, especially if you decide to tell him about your Asperger's Syndrome. Signs that a co-worker will make a good work buddy include:

- Patience when answering your questions; they don't say, "I'm surprised you don't know that," or "It's obvious," or "Weren't you paying attention?"

- Volunteering information that is important for you to know, like things that annoy your supervisor, who is trustworthy, or who to go to with questions

- Introducing you to other people in the company

- Making sure that you are invited to lunches with your department or team members, or to social events outside the office

Once you have identified a colleague with these characteristics, it is not necessary to ask that he or she become your work buddy. This will happen naturally over time. Be careful not to overwhelm this person with questions and requests for advice. Build the relationship through interaction and becoming friendly.

Express your gratitude for the assistance you receive (e.g. "Thanks, Bill, for filling me in on the situation with Steve"). Be alert for ways to reciprocate, such as offering to pitch in if your buddy has a lot of work, bringing them a cup of coffee or taking the person to lunch. You do not need to "keep score," that is, do something for the person every time they do something for you. If you are uncertain of appropriate ways to show appreciation, talk the situation over with someone outside of work.

How to Be a Team Player

"Talk less, listen and think about what others are saying."
IP Project Manager, age 61

The ability to work effectively with others is a necessary skill. But what exactly makes someone a good team player?

Being a "team player" means working collaboratively with other people to reach a common goal. A team can be comprised of people in your department, individuals from different parts of the company who are collaborating on a project (this is sometimes referred to as a cross-functional team), or the members of a specific committee.

Each team member needs to understand how their expertise and skills contribute to the project's success. As in any group, different people will have different needs, values, personality styles and personal objectives. At times this results in team conflicts.

A stated team goal such as, "create a top-quality widget," carries with it all of the unstated ambitions of the people involved. The VP of Manufacturing might see the objective as, "Create a top-quality widget ... but keep production costs low." The Director of Marketing thinks, "Create a top-quality widget ... that will be ready in time for our fall sales campaign." The Vice President of Sales hears, "Create a top-quality widget ... that has features that our customers will buy so that I will earn my quarterly bonus." If the concerns and priorities of team members are too diverse or clash, it will be very difficult for the group to function cohesively, reach consensus and make decisions.

An essential aspect of teamwork is listening to and respecting the ideas of others—whether you agree with them or not! Pay attention when other people are speaking so that you can understand their problems and point-of-view. This information will give you a sense of the big picture and will assist you in presenting your ideas in a way that addresses the concerns of others in the group.

Allow others to finish speaking before you respond. Do not interject negative comments or correct minor mistakes. Others will perceive this as condescending and arrogant.

Brian readily admitted his contempt for what he called the "shallow" corporate expressions used by his colleagues. It wasn't until his performance review that he realized the impact of his sarcastic comments on his co-workers. "People don't think that you want to be part of the team," he supervisor said. Brian decided to make positive statements instead. Now if someone mentions "creating synergies," he responds with, "Here's how I think we can get the most out of our combined efforts."

Nancy's command of her employer's complex internal systems and processes was lauded throughout her division. She had also earned a reputation as difficult to work with and as a poor team player. Nancy frequently interrupted people with comments like, "That won't work" or "We've tried that before." "But I know their ideas won't work," Nancy protested during one of our coaching sessions. "Why should I waste time letting them go on and on?"

By interrupting, Nancy was unintentionally sending a message to others that she didn't respect their ideas or think that they had anything important to contribute. Nancy later found out that some co-workers interpreted her remarks to mean that she thought *they* were stupid.

Nancy agreed to experiment with not interrupting for the next week. This was especially difficult when she was listening to the junior members of the department. At first, Nancy noticed her rising feelings of impatience as they proposed solutions that she knew would not work. By the third day, she realized that listening enabled her to identify the areas where these employees needed additional training.

Clear communication is particularly important when you work on a team. Think what would happen on a baseball diamond or a football field, if the players had no idea what their teammates were doing. The same principal applies at work. It is a mistake to assume that other people see a situation the same way that you do, or that they will draw the same conclusions. Pete was assigned to an emergency project and presumed that his co-workers would know that his regular work would be late. His co-workers, however, assumed that everything was on schedule because Pete didn't tell them there would be delays! At his performance review, Pete was described as a poor team player.

Team interaction goes two ways. In addition to keeping colleagues informed about your work, you should make an effort to find out what they are working on as well. This demonstrates a team orientation and shows how your work fits into the whole. I have had multiple clients tell me that once they stopped tuning out at meetings, they were amazed to learn how co-worker's projects had an effect on their own.

Finally, good team players express enthusiasm, even if they don't always feel it. This is not to suggest that you try to impress people with obviously faked, highly animated behaviors. You can express enthusiasm by asking questions, making supportive comments, sharing helpful ideas and listening intently when people speak.

Company culture dictates standards of teamwork. Observe how, when and where your colleagues interact. Do they socialize for a few minutes before starting meetings or do people enter the conference room and get down to business right away? Do most people in your work group eat lunch at their desks or do they eat together in the lunch room? Do they get together after work? As much as possible, match your level of social interaction with that of your teammates.

PEOPLE WHO ARE DESCRIBED AS "HARD TO WORK WITH ..."

- Make lots of negative comments
- Refuse to participate in discussions
- Interrupt to disagree or correct someone
- Resist or challenge the ideas of others consistently

NT TIP: There are times when it is acceptable and desirable to disagree with colleagues. State your opinion in neutral terms, such as "I see the situation differently," or "Here's how I look at it." Judgmental phrases like "That's dumb," or "Anyone can see that" make people defensive and less inclined to listen to your point of view.

CHAPTER FOUR

Managing Your Career

Evan's life-long passion was music. After earning a master's degree at one of the finest music programs in the country, he began his career in audio engineering.

He was shocked when his work was rejected outright, since he believed that he had followed his supervisor's instructions to the letter. Additionally, working in a small office surrounded by other people for 50 to 60 hours a week was proving to be a tremendous strain. He began to intentionally alienate his colleagues by making negative comments about their hobbies and interests. He was fired within six months.

His next position seemed ideal because he was able to work in nearly total isolation. Once, he didn't have to speak to anyone else in the company for two weeks. Then he began reporting to a new supervisor. He was instructed to create "emotional content" and "give customers a religious experience," which were completely meaningless directives to Evan. He was fired within three months.

At the next job, he was again flummoxed by responsibilities that included becoming a "product evangelist" and "leveraging the brand." Discouraged, he withdrew his energy from the job and was fired yet again.

When his fourth position ended the same way, Evan realized that he needed to make changes. His employment goal was to earn a steady income and stay with a company long enough to earn a promotion. He asked a former co-worker to help him figure out what was going wrong.

"It was then that I realized that my job was to execute ideas from the creative team," Evan said, "and that if I wanted to stay employed, I had to stop ignoring their directions." When he landed his next job, he followed instructions and also worked to improve his communication skills. "It took extraordinary effort, but I started talking to people during the day and made positive comments in meetings." He also learned about working as part of a team. "If another department got their specs to me late, I couldn't assume that everyone else would know that my work would be late as a result." He also realized that if people didn't comment on a proposal, it didn't mean that they agreed with it. He began following up and asking colleagues for their feedback.

After more than four years with this company, during which he earned a promotion and received two salary increases, Evan accepted a more challenging opportunity with another firm. "This is the first time that the choice to move to another company was mine," he says.

There are two parts to managing your career. The first is meeting expectations and interacting effectively with colleagues so that you will remain steadily employed. Multiple job losses not only impact your earning power, but can lead to a loss of self-esteem, depression and stress.

The second part is professional development. This includes keeping your skills up-to-date or improving them, being aware of significant changes in your industry, creating a professional network and building on your strengths.

This chapter offers ideas for how to manage your career.

Build on Your Strengths

"It's easy to be negative and think about all the things you find difficult. Try and be positive instead and remind yourself of all the things you can do and the things that you can learn to do. You are not disabled, you just have differing abilities."

Manufacturer's Representative, age 39

Building on your areas of strength is important career advice for everyone. If you are someone with Asperger's Syndrome, it is an important career strategy. Let's face it, you will not be able to compete for jobs based on salesmanship, political savvy, or leadership. However, you can compete on the strengths of the Asperger mind. These include:

sustained concentration and focus; extensive knowledge of specialized fields; innovative thinking; accuracy and an eye for detail. Personal characteristics such as persistence, honesty and loyalty are benefits to every employer.

Within the workplace, neurotypicals are multitasking generalists. They have skills in several different areas and can adapt rather easily to change. As an individual with Asperger's Syndrome, you are among the experts and technicians of the workplace. You tend to develop greater expertise within a narrow area.

Specialisterne ("the specialists") is an innovative, for-profit software testing company based in Denmark. Its business model is based on utilizing the cognitive strengths of people with Asperger's Syndrome and high functioning autism. Specialisterne specifically hires people on the autism spectrum because their focus, attention to detail and precision makes them better software testers than most neurotypicals. Specialisterne's clients include Microsoft and Oracle. It has received international attention, and founder Thorkil Sonne, whose son has Asperger's Syndrome, has created a non-profit foundation named the Specialist People Foundation. Its goal is to create one million jobs for so-called "Specialist People" around the world. (To learn more, visit www.specialisterne.com.)

Michael Burry is a physician-turned-hedge-fund-manager who has Asperger's Syndrome. In 2004, he became interested in the bond market. He was able to predict the coming sub-prime mortgage meltdown years before anybody else saw it coming. "He didn't talk to anyone about what became his new obsession: he just sat alone in his office ... and read books and articles and financial filings," writes Michael Lewis in *The Big Short: Inside the Doomsday Machine*.[1]

You may not work for Specialisterne or reach the prominence of Michael Burry. However you can look for ways to capitalize on your strengths so that they outweigh your limitations in the eyes of an employer.

---

[1] *The Big Short: Inside the Doomsday Machine*, ©2010, Michael Lewis, excerpted in the article *Betting on the Blind Side* in the April, 2010 issue of Vanity Fair magazine.

I have worked with clients in their 40's and 50's who have no idea where their talents lie. Often they are in careers that emphasize their challenges instead of their assets. Even when this is apparent to the individual, some are so uncomfortable with change that they remain in very difficult jobs that drain their energy and leave them in constant fear of being fired.

By continually developing your strengths, you can very likely compensate for your weaknesses in communication and organization. Several of my clients have earned the respect of their co-workers due to their superior technical ability. Others have found jobs where the accuracy and quality of their work makes up for it taking them longer to produce it.

Your strengths can be negotiating tools as well. One young man convinced a potential employer to overlook a requirement for one year of work experience by demonstrating his in-depth knowledge of a particular kind of machinery.

There are many different career tests that measure skills, aptitudes and preferences. Some are available at no charge online and others must be administered for a fee by a licensed career counselor. You can also create a profile of your strengths by writing down the following:

- Talents, which are the things that you are naturally good at, such as writing, drawing, teaching, researching, analyzing, designing, etc.
- Skills, which are specific competencies that you learn and develop over time, such as accounting, computer programming, oil painting, medical coding, welding, etc.
- Personal characteristics, which include qualities such as honesty, persistence, intelligence, patience, creativity, and loyalty.
- Education, such as formal degrees, certificate programs, apprenticeships, attendance at workshops and conferences, as well as self-taught knowledge.
- Personal experience in situations where you have applied your talents and skills.

Once you understand what your strengths and abilities are, you can formulate a plan for building on them. Denise works as an occupational therapist at a private clinic. She is very good at teaching. Denise developed a workshop that was so popular among patients that the director of the clinic decided to offer it to the public. That resulted in new clients for the clinic and an expanded role for Denise, who is creating more educational programs.

Developing your talents and skills is something that you do over the course of your career. Keep your skills current and look for ways that your abilities can be used to fill a need at work. Sharon noticed that her manager spent a lot of time training people on a complicated data entry process. She volunteered to write an instructional manual, an activity that utilized her writing skills and ability to break complex material into simple steps.

There are many opportunities outside of your job to develop your talents as well. Non-profit agencies and professional associations often rely on skilled volunteers to assist on different kinds of projects. People have created successful blogs and Web sites based on their expertise in a particular subject area.

One caveat: when building on your strengths be sure that you do not neglect other critical business skills. You probably will not be able to work in isolation, like Michael Burry. Every improvement you make in communication, organization and time management will pay off many times over.

Why You Need to Network

"Social skills are the key to success in life. Lack of them will cost you everything—friends, lovers and a career in something you love."
Industrial Hygienist, age 50

This is a tale of two clients. Both work in the high tech industry. Both were laid off unexpectedly. Joe went home and immediately began searching the job boards and sending out resumes; lots and lots of resumes. Steven went home and sent out emails to about 20 of his business contacts. Within 48 hours, one of those contacts told him about an opening at a company that had tried to recruit Steven previously. Steven contacted the company, and two weeks after being laid off accepted a job offer and was preparing to move out of state.

During week four of Joe's search, he met with a recruiter and realized that he could not supply three references, as requested. His emails to former co-workers bounced back, and when he did manage to locate them at their new companies, his queries went unanswered. It had been 3 years since he had spoken with one and 4 ½ years since he had spoken with the other. "They may not even remember me," he thought.

Maura's tale: She was unhappy with her graphic design job. She had worked for the same company for 9 years and wondered if she could transfer her skills to another, higher paying industry. Unsure of what kind of qualifications she would need, Maura thought about taking an expensive certificate program. She felt stuck and wished that there was someone with industry experience with whom she could discuss options.

Finally, Phil's tale: Recently he had been assigned to handle the programming of a new, innovative piece of software. It was a high visibility project, one that could put him in line for a promotion. Phil's supervisor has commented more than once about the slow pace of the work. Phil assured him that everything was moving according to schedule; however, he was actually slipping behind because of difficulties with the new programming tools he was using. No one else in the company had experience with them and his calls to manufacturer's technical support staff weren't solving the problems.

These stories illustrate that the value of networking goes beyond finding a job. Your contacts can help with career research, make you aware of new resources, and offer advice about how to solve various problems.

Despite all of these positives, you may still cringe at the idea of networking, envisioning yourself standing in a room full of strangers, unsure of who to approach or what to say. However there are other ways to establish meaningful connections with people in your field.

Chapter Two of this book includes a section on how to set up an informational interview, which is a form of networking used for career research. In this chapter, the focus is on networking for the purpose of creating and maintaining a business network that will be useful throughout your career.

Every profession has associations or trade groups which can be excellent channels for meeting people in your field or industry. These groups typically hold monthly meetings that feature a period of socializing followed by a presentation. They may also sponsor conferences, special events or training programs, and host online forums or groups. Prospective members can usually attend one meeting for free or for a flat fee in order to evaluate the group. If you decide to join, your employer might pay the membership fee. Associations provide structure and ready-made topics for discussion that facilitate social interaction. You might serve on a volunteer committee, which allows you to make contact with members within the context of an official "job."

Do some advance preparation before you attend an association event. Visit the group's Web site to familiarize yourself with its mission, history and activities. Prepare questions to ask people during the networking period, such as, "How long have you been a member of this association?," "Are you familiar with tonight's speaker?," and "What kind of work do you do?" If you are very anxious about talking to people you don't know, plan to arrive just in time for the formal presentation. Challenge yourself to speak to the person seated to your right and left, even if you ask just a single question. Practice builds confidence and over time, the conversing will get easier.

Joining a professional association is not the only way to build a network. You can find industry-specific online discussion groups to participate in for free. You make connections by asking questions, replying to people's questions and starting your own discussion threads.

If you write well, submit articles for publication in trade magazines or on industry Web sites, or start a blog. Insightful, well-written material can build your recognition and credibility in a field and can lead to job offers.

Speaking at industry conferences and events is another way to make connections. Association Web sites and trade magazines often post listings of up-coming conferences. Event producers plan their programs nine months to a year in advance, so submit your proposal early.

It is also wise to stay in touch with former co-workers you got along well with previously. You can connect through online business networking sites, such as LinkedIn. After creating a profile, you invite individuals you know to join your network, and can send out status updates on a periodic basis. People may invite you to join their networks as well. When you post an update, make sure that it is business related. Avoid posts about your personal relationships ("I'm getting a divorce"), and negative remarks about other people or your company ("My boss is a complete jerk;" "This company has terrible benefits"). Appropriate topics are: announcing a promotion or a new job; forwarding a link to an interesting business article; mentioning an industry conference that you are attending; etc.

Read the updates that others post, and respond with a note when appropriate (e.g. "Congratulations on your promotion;" "Good luck in your new job;" "Enjoyed the article you mentioned").

Online networking is an informal way to maintain connections. There may be one or several people with whom you wish to establish stronger relationships. A good way to do this is to invite them for lunch or a cup of coffee. Your outreach does not have to be frequent. An invitation every few months or once a year is usually enough (unless, of course, you both enjoy getting together more often). It is important that you express a genuine interest in learning about how the person is doing. If you contact people only when you need a favor, they will not want to stay in touch with you.

While some people have business relationships that span decades, it is more likely that you will lose touch with some individuals over two or three years. The important thing is that they are replaced by new people who you have met and added to your network.

Having an interest in your work makes it easier to attend industry events and make contact with colleagues. Some people who have little interest in socializing discover that they enjoy interacting with other professionals to discuss industry news and share ideas. If you are currently working in an area that is not satisfying, find ways to interact with people who share a personal interest of yours. This can also be a way to network. Lee, for example, joined a book group for science fiction enthusiasts. A few months later, one of the members told her about a job opening at a shop that specializes in science fiction books and merchandise. She now works there, assisting customers and contributing articles to store's Web site.

Networking requires consistent effort over time, so choose activities that you will continue. Attending a single association meeting, or writing one blog post every few months, will not yield results. Do at least one thing that involves face-to-face meetings, as this is how the most meaningful connections are made.

Anatomy of a 30-Second Elevator Speech

An "elevator speech" (aka "elevator pitch," "commercial") is a brief summary of who you are and what you do. It is used as a means of introduction at various kinds of business events. The elevator pitch is so named because you should be able to say it within roughly the same brief period of time that an elevator ride would take.

Job seekers use elevator pitches to describe their qualifications and explain what kind of work they want. Individuals who are employed use their "commercial" at networking events, professional conferences and other in business situations.

The length of an elevator speech varies from 30 seconds or less up to 2 minutes. Support groups for people who are unemployed and business networking groups often give attendees one or two minutes each to explain what they do, and make a request. The request might be for job leads, potential customers to contact, ideas for marketing a service, etc. When you are introducing yourself to someone, your summary should be about 30 seconds. Professionals usually prepare several versions of their speech to use for different occasions.

For job seekers, the basic format of an elevator speech is to state your name, what you do, what are your skills and what type of work you seek. For example:

- Job seeker, brief: "My name is Beth Jones and I develop business-to-business marketing programs for new customer acquisition. I am looking for a position at a mid-size business publisher."

- Job seeker, more detailed: "My name is Beth Jones and I have 12 years of experience developing customer acquisition programs for business-to-business publishers. I utilize direct marketing, social media and telemarketing to generate new sales. My most recent campaign brought in over $1 million in revenue. My ideal job is at a mid-size publisher in the Boston area."

The format is similar for individuals who are seeking referrals or business contacts:

- "My name is Mike Smith and I am with Corporate Photography Studios. We specialize in photography for annual reports, corporate brochures and Web sites. My clients include ACME Company and LM Widgets. Recently I was at The Town Machinery Company photographing 12 members of the management team and their new factory. I am looking for the names of marketing directors at companies with 250 employees or more."

When introducing yourself to individuals during the networking portion of a business event, you should use a less formal, more conversational style: "Hello, my name is Bob Johnson. I'm a programmer at ABC Software." Often people will exchange comments and questions for 3 to 5 turns, for example:

BOB: "Hello, my name is Bob Johnson. I'm a programmer at ABC Software. We specialize in applications for media development."

MARY: "Hi, Bob. I'm Mary Wright and I head the marketing group at DataComputation Associates. We consult to Fortune 1000 companies. Is this your first time at a Tech Professionals

Association meeting?"

BOB: "Yes. I am eager to meet some other people in the field. A colleague at work spoke highly of this group. Have you been a member long?"

MARY: "For 3 years and I have met a lot of very interesting and talented people here. What kind of projects do you work on?"

BOB: "Right now I am writing code for some new multimedia software. You don't happen to know of someone who has worked with the MegaBuilder program, do you?"

Experiment with your "pitch" until you are comfortable saying it. Some people prefer to use a lot of descriptive language ("I am a technology-savvy, results-oriented marketing manager...") while others are more factual. Practice so that you sound confident, but not robotic.

A Primer on Office Politics

"Politics is probably more important for success than you think it is."
IT Project Manager, age 62

For many people, the term office politics conjures up images of a greedy, back-stabbing executive, who will do anything to get to the top, or the butt-kissing underling who wins a promotion, despite having no brains or talent. Although the majority of NTs dislike office politics, they participate in it anyway. For the majority of people with Asperger's Syndrome, office politics is thoroughly confusing and something to avoid.

Like it or not, office politics is a fact of working life. It is the unspoken rules about who has power in an organization, and how things get done. Yes, there are some people who play political games strictly for their own gain, often with poor results. Most, though, pay attention to these unspoken rules of organizational life because it makes their jobs easier.

It bears repeating that NTs are socially focused. Their group orientation means that struggles over where one fits within the hierarchy of the unit are common. This is why success at work requires more than having the talent and skills to do a job. Individuals need to fit in to their organization's culture and figure out who has the power to get things done.

Like people, companies each have their own personality, known as corporate culture. This does not necessarily match characteristics that are described in a marketing brochure or on a company Web site. Corporate culture is based on shared values, the beliefs that people share about what is important. Values are what drive actions. You can learn a lot about company culture by observing what behaviors are rewarded. A company may claim to have a culture of innovation and creativity, yet it rewards consistency and preservation of the status quo.

It is possible for departments within a company to have distinct cultures that reflect the values of employees in that group, and not necessarily the values of the company. Managers have a tendency to hire people whose values are similar to their own. A bottom line oriented general manager is likely to hire staff members who are focused on growing revenue and maximizing profit. A general manager who is quality oriented will hire people who won't cut corners to meet sales targets. Neither culture is better or worse than the other; they are simply different. The first company might produce quality products, but bonuses are based on meeting sales targets. The second company might tolerate delays in order to release top-quality products. Corporate culture rewards employees who most help the company succeed.

These are more examples of contrasting company cultures:

- Hierarchical vs. collaborative
- Emphasis on tasks and getting things done vs. interpersonal relationships and how things get done
- Fixed rules and processes vs. flexible rules and processes
- Business focus where people's private lives stay private vs. relationship-oriented where people have on and off the job camaraderie
- Analytic, linear problem solving vs. intuitive, creative problem solving (Microsoft versus Apple)

- Slow paced, static environment vs. fast paced, rapidly changing environment

A company's culture can change over time, sometimes dramatically. There may be a rapid influx of new employees due to rapid growth, or a natural turnover of employees over several years. A significant event, such as a merger or acquisition, the death of a founder or other senior executive, regulatory change, or new market dynamics like greater price competition, can force a change in values.

Understanding office politics also means figuring out who has power and authority and how they use them to get things done. Job title can be an unreliable indicator of whether an individual has power or not. In every company there are two kinds of organizational charts. One is the official diagram that shows who reports to whom, the relationships between departments, and where responsibilities lie. The other more important one is the unofficial chain of command. This one reveals who has real authority. An individual's authority is typically based on who they know, their specialized expertise or institutional knowledge, or their ability to influence or help others. For example, a busy company president may give control of his calendar to his executive assistant. If you have dealings with the president, it helps to have a good relationship with his executive assistant, or you might find that meetings with the boss are hard to schedule.

Employees who possess specialized expertise may be given certain "perks" as an incentive to stay at the firm. Staff members who have worked at a company for many years amass a wealth of valuable institutional knowledge. Their power lies in their understanding of various processes, procedures, and people; in other words, how things really work. There are the individuals who make it their business to learn the needs of others in the organization. They use this information to influence the decisions of others.

Office Politics in Action

If you think that awareness of office politics is important only to people who work in big companies and want to climb the corporate ladder, think again. During high school, Mike had a part-time job at a local gas station. His passion was automobiles and he wanted desperately to learn how to fix them. During his breaks, Mike was in the garage, handing tools to the mechanics and watching them work. When he heard the station owner say, "I'm getting hungry," Mike offered to pick up lunch for him and the other mechanics (he did not pay for the lunches; he collected money from each person and walked to the sandwich shop to pick up the food when it was ready).

If Mike's motive had been disingenuous, helping the mechanics in order to get some kind of special treatment, it would have backfired. However, the station owner and the mechanics sensed his genuine interest in fixing cars. Even though he wasn't consciously aware of it, Mike used his understanding of who had power in the gas station to influence the right people. Instead of hanging out with the other pump attendants talking about sports, Mike built relationships with the mechanics and the owner of the station. That summer, Mike was working full time as a mechanic's apprentice.

Awareness of office politics tells you: who has the real authority, how decisions get made, what behaviors are rewarded, what is really important, who can champion your projects and ideas, and when and with whom you need to compromise. As you begin to grasp these unspoken rules, events that seemed random or mystifying begin to make sense. You know who to go to for help. You stop taking the actions of others personally. The big picture becomes clearer: decisions that seemed contrary to stated business objectives make sense. You can see how people set themselves up for promotions by increasing their value to the company.

Katy and Suzanne worked as technical documentation writers for a large software company. Their job was to write clear, concise copy for manuals and on-line help that explain how to use a software product. The job required that they work closely with the developers who created the software.

Katy's writing skills were consistently described as excellent and exceeding expectations. Although she didn't work as quickly, her finished product was so thorough and accurate that editing her work took a fraction of the time to edit others. Katy liked her job and each morning headed straight to her computer and began typing. She often ate lunch at her desk. She frequently got into heated debates with the developers about the features and functionality of their products. Katy admitted that she enjoyed these discussions, "because usually I know more than they do and win."

Suzanne, on the other hand, did not have the same depth of technical knowledge or writing skills. However, Suzanne got along well with both the developers and the editors, often joining them for lunch. She built relationships by filling them in on non-confidential information from the strategy meetings. She stayed late to fix a glaring error that one of the editors made, before Cory, the department supervisor, could find out about it.

Over the past quarter, company layoffs resulted in the loss of one editor and major cutbacks in the budget for freelance help. Everyone in the documentation department was feeling the pressure to get projects completed on time. It puzzled Katy that editors would stay late to work on Suzanne's projects, but not on hers. "My last two projects were for new product releases," Katy explained, "and that is where most of the revenue comes from. I don't understand why editors would waste extra time reviewing Suzanne's updates." The developers and editors were reciprocating for Suzanne's help by handling her projects first whenever possible.

During this period, Katy also noticed that Suzanne was spending more and more time in closed door meetings with Cory. Suzanne was being invited to participate in monthly strategy meetings with the product and marketing managers. It was announced that Suzanne would accompany Cory to a major industry conference in the fall.

"Cory likes Suzanne and he doesn't like me," Katy said to Ellen, a junior editor with whom she was friendly. "That's why he's letting her go to the conference."

"Haven't you heard?" Ellen said, "Cory is taking a job in the product development group. Suzanne is going to be the documentation supervisor."

"I didn't see any announcement," Katy replied, stunned.

"There isn't going to be an announcement until next month," said Ellen. "Cory told two of the developers, and one of them told Ann in product development, who told me. Don't say anything, okay?"

On the surface, Suzanne's promotion seems absurd. Her writing and technical skills are not as strong as Katy's. She didn't work on the new product releases. She hadn't worked for the company as long as Katy.

But, from the perspective of office politics, Suzanne's promotion makes perfect sense. She was perceived as a team player. The company culture placed a lot of value on group consensus and interaction, which Suzanne did well.

Cory noticed the good relationships that Suzanne had with her workmates. When he accepted a new position in the company, he immediately began grooming Suzanne to take over his job. The more politically astute members of the documentation department guessed that Suzanne's presence at the industry conference meant that she was going to get a promotion.

Even Ellen, who had only been with the company for five months, knew to utilize the company grapevine to find out news before it was announced. The grapevine is the information exchange that happens through informal networks.

Katy's lack of political awareness made it hard for her to influence others. As a result, her projects were not treated with the same sense of urgency as Suzanne's. It also kept her out of the running for a promotion. The software developers did not share Katy's enjoyment of the product debates. Several felt that she was condescending in her critiques and one had requested not to work with her in the future. By not joining her colleagues for lunch, Katy missed opportunities to form better relationships and learn more about their concerns and how she could help.

NT TIP: Joining people in your department or work group for lunch is not a waste of time. The conversation may start off with small talk, but usually turns to business matters.

Eric was chronically irritated by what he saw as capricious behavior by his colleagues. "The rules are not followed and arbitrarily broken at the whim of a co-worker or manager," he explained. What Eric didn't realize is that decisions can be politically motivated, and can appear contrary to stated business objectives. A manager who is in line for a promotion might decide to delay a not-quite-ready product release. A marketing director might support a sales department initiative because he knows that he will need help from the sales team. As in chess, people make moves and counter moves to win the game.

You may be wondering how, as a person with Asperger's Syndrome, you can ever hope to become savvy at office politics. Understanding the motives of other people is a struggle, you often miss the implied meaning of what people say, and are uncomfortable with interpersonal interaction. It may seem that you have to lie about your motives.

You do not need to become a person who wields political power in your organization. Instead, you can develop enough awareness of office politics to make your job easier. This can be as basic as making yourself available to help others who are behind on projects; taking an interest in what your colleagues are doing; and being supportive when they have professional or personal problems.

These are suggestions for increasing your awareness of office politics:

- Become an astute observer. Begin watching the daily interactions in the lunch room and during breaks to get an idea of who has interpersonal connections with whom. If necessary, keep a chart of people who frequently talk together (but be discreet about it). Pay attention to people in your own department. How do they act? Is there a lot of chatter and camaraderie or is everyone working silently at their desks?

When people need answers or assistance, who do they go to for help? Who gets attention at meetings?

- Once you understand the social networks, look for people or situations that can help you. The peer who is friendly and patient when answering people's questions might be able to give you suggestions on how to work more efficiently.

- Talking to people is essential to learning about office politics. Just be sure to do so in a politically correct way. Even though it is ubiquitous, company politicking is usually not openly acknowledged. Do not ask, "Who has the real power in this company?" or "What are the office politics like here?" Ask instead, "How would you describe the company's culture?", "What are the primary concerns of the product development group?" or "What are the top three priorities over the next six months?"

- Ask a co-worker you trust to act as your office politics interpreter. Perhaps this person is your work buddy (see Chapter Three for information on a work buddy). You do not need to reveal that you have Asperger's Syndrome. This person is someone with whom you have developed a rapport, so you can be direct with your request ("I'm not good at office politics. Would you clue me in on how things work here?").

- Accept that political motives, not logic, can drive decisions, and use this awareness to learn when to compromise. If you rely only on official rules, policies and procedures you will become frustrated.

- There are many business books that explain the dynamics of office politics. Find one that you like and enlist the help of an NT to help you apply the book's concepts to your situation. If you are really inspired, study organizational development to gain insight into corporate culture.

What If Things Get Ugly?

A company's culture can become one of in-fighting, back-stabbing and never-ending political intrigue. Sometimes, innocent people get caught in the middle of the battles, and this can make the work environment very stressful and unproductive. Unless the politics directly affects your ability to do your work or your job security, try to stay out of the fray. It is likely that 99% of the gossip you hear will be wrong. Don't take sides; focus on your assigned tasks. There may be very little that you can do to better the situation and your best alternative may be to seek employment elsewhere.

Talk to someone, like a coach or career counselor, who can help you explore your options. Resist the urge to simply quit. It will make it harder for you to find another job, and make a bad impression on your employer. You never know when you could be working with a former colleague again. Whenever possible, leave an employer on good terms.

How to Handle Conflicts and Disagreements

Dan was considered a brilliant engineer and was respected for his vast knowledge of his company's products and internal processes. Co-workers commented that Dan always seemed to be two or three steps ahead of them, able to quickly size up a proposal and determine whether it was feasible. A 16-year veteran of the organization, Dan had amassed a wealth of institutional knowledge and could recall details that others had long forgotten.

Two years before the company had gone through a major reorganization. Dan had never fully been able to adapt to the changes in management and culture. Although he reported to the same supervisor, Dan worked on an almost daily basis with a manager he did not like or respect. Dan believed that the manager deliberately tried to make him look incompetent. The manager would promise to get information to Dan by a certain date and not deliver. Their philosophies about product designs were quite different and their discussions sometimes turned into shouting matches.

Dan was also expected to collaborate with product development, marketing and sales personnel. Their lack of basic engineering knowledge frustrated Dan to the point that he would lose his temper, curse, or simply walk out of meetings. He would routinely preface answers to a colleague's questions with, "I can't believe you don't know that," or "you've worked here long enough to know..."

His second post-reorganization performance review was a complete shock to Dan. He was told that he would not receive a long-anticipated promotion because of his abrasive interpersonal style. "It isn't so much what you say as how you say it," his supervisor said. "People feel that they are being criticized and belittled. You need to be collaborating."

Jill was one of two paralegals in a small law firm. She and her peer, Susan, each worked for two attorneys and were expected to help each other with assignments when the firm was busy. Jill didn't particularly like Susan, who was loud, careless with her work and prone to taking extra long lunch breaks. Still, they had managed to work together for nearly a year without incident.

One afternoon Allen, an attorney, asked Jill if she knew were Susan was. "She's at lunch," Jill replied. "Oh?" said Allen, looking at his watch. "Would you tell her to stop by my office as soon as she gets in?" he asked.

After he left, Jill looked at her watch and noticed that it was 1:40pm. Susan had left for lunch at about 12:15; she was already almost a half hour late.

When Susan finally came in at about 1:50, Jill relayed the conversation with Allen. "Why did you tell him I was lunch?" Susan asked in an angry tone, "Now he's going to be mad because I'm late. Thanks a lot," she added and stormed off.

The exchange left Jill anxious and upset. Why wouldn't she tell Allen that Susan was at lunch, if that's where she was? Why was Susan so angry at her for being honest? Jill had no idea what to do next and spent about 15 minutes crying in the ladies room.

Disagreements are a common part of working life. They can range in intensity from minor differences of opinion to major conflicts. The causes can be many. In Dan's case it wasn't so much what he said as the way he said it that had his colleagues believing that he didn't respect them. Jill was caught in a misunderstanding with Susan, who wrongly assumed that Jill had told Allen that she had been gone since 12:15.

Allen had seen Susan leaving the building at a quarter past noon.

Differing personality styles can cause friction between co-workers, as can contradictory goals and divergent values. The goal of the research department might be to produce an in-depth, insightful report. The goal of the marketing department might be to have a finished product to sell. Any delays will cause tension between the two departments. The people in research will feel pressured to produce a product that is not comprehensive, while the people in marketing will feel pressured to generate orders. The vice president might value quick, decisive decision making while his manager values the careful evaluation of lots of data. The vice president will be impatient with the manager, and the manager will feel pressured by the vice president.

Whether disagreements can be resolved before they become emotionally-charged conflicts depends on a number of factors. Unrealistic expectations or conflicting directives from senior executives can create workplaces that are filled with fear and mistrust. In-fighting between department or division heads can stall projects and lead to anger and hurt feelings.

There is not a lot that you can do about management conflicts, unless you are at the same management level or are already a trusted advisor to both. However, there are techniques that you can learn to handle interpersonal disagreements and conflicts between you and your co-workers.

Remember that the purpose of your interactions with others is the fulfillment of business objectives. You do not need to personally like a co-worker to work with him, nor do you have to agree with everything he says or does. Be prepared to interact with people whose perspectives, personalities, goals and values differ from yours.

Keep in mind the social orientation of NTs. They want their opinions to be heard and respected. They do not want to look foolish, especially in front of staff members and their boss. They tend to seek consensus and are often willing to compromise to maintain harmony. Dan, like many of my clients, didn't think about this and, as a result, his manager and colleagues felt belittled and criticized.

As long as you are not overstepping your authority, it is okay to disagree with co-workers, give them feedback or challenge their ideas. Examples of overstepping authority include: ignoring company policies or procedures; performing tasks that are not in your job description; giving instructions to people who don't report to you; offering unsolicited comments or advice about projects in other departments; or attempting tasks that are outside of your skills, abilities or experience.

When you give feedback or disagree, avoid statements that imply judgment, or that reflect your opinion about what happened and how you or others reacted. For example, the statement, "If you had listened to the instructions we would have been done by now," implies judgment of an individual. The unspoken meaning is, "If you had done what you were supposed to, the project would have been completed on time." The statement, "No one could understand your logic," is evaluative. It implies that others share this opinion because the presenter didn't articulate his thoughts well.

Statements that imply judgment or that are evaluative make people defensive. Instead of hearing the content of your message, they concentrate on protecting themselves from a perceived attack. If your words don't make people defensive, they are able to listen to what you have to say.

To do this, state your opinions or beliefs using neutral language and "I" statements rather than "you" statements. For example: "I see it a different way;" "I hear what you are saying, but my experience is different;" "Let me share my concerns."

If a co-worker says or does something that you find upsetting, do not react until you have had a chance to calm down. You can say something like, "I am upset right now and want to think about what happened, before we discuss it."

Put a single interaction into perspective (get help with this if you need it). Consider the history that you have had with the other person. Is the individual usually friendly and helpful? Have you gotten along well in the past? Has a similar incident happened before? Everyone can have a bad day, so if someone's behavior is out of character, it might be because they have a personal or professional problem.

Think also about the severity of the upsetting event. Is it an inconsequential difference of opinion or a serious dispute ... or something in between? Putting the situation into proportion will help you to make the right decision about how to handle it.

Is it possible that you have misunderstood the other person's words or actions? Think about the context of the situation. Perhaps the other person was making a joke, teasing you, or trying to be helpful. If you are not sure, ask: "I'm not sure what you mean," "Was that a joke?" or "I'm confused; are you upset about something?"

Unresolved disagreements and conflicts can worsen over time, so it is important to take action to correct the situation. Speak directly with the individual first, in a private location. The following 5-step model outlines an effective way to give someone feedback in a non-judgmental way.

- Step 1: Describe the situation using specific, factual (not judgmental or evaluative) language
- Step 2: Describe the impact of the situation on the business
- Step 3: Explain how it effects you and your work
- Step 4: Explain, in detail, what you would have the person do differently
- Step 5: Reach agreement

Dan used this model the next time that his manager did not follow through with promised information:

- *"When the specs are late..."* (factual description)
- *"I have to revise the plan for the review committee..."* (impact of situation on business)
- *"This eats up about an hour of my time..."* (impact on you)
- *"I'd appreciate it if you would only give me deadlines that you know you can meet..."* (what you want the person to do)
- *"Is this reasonable?"* (check for agreement)

Do not omit the last step. People are more likely to follow through if they agree with what they are being asked to do. This question gives the other person a chance to raise their concerns so that the situation can be resolved.

Practice this model until you get comfortable with it. You do not have to use the exact phrasing shown here. Use words that feel natural to you. If you sound disingenuous or rehearsed, people will not respond favorably. It can be helpful to write down what you want to say and practice it a few times.

This kind of feedback should be given within 24 hours of an incident. Unless there is a very specific or important reason for doing so, avoid bringing up events that happened days or weeks ago. This can make it seem like you are harping on the past or intentionally trying to demean someone.

If your efforts to resolve the situation are not successful, or you are unsure about what to do, speak with your supervisor or work buddy. Use factual, neutral language, for example: "I'm confused about a situation with Bill," or "Jane and I don't see eye to eye and it's affecting our projects."

When Susan returned from her meeting with Allan, she apologized to Jill for the misunderstanding. Jill accepted the apology, grateful to know that she had not done anything wrong. Still concerned, Jill spoke with her supervisor and they agreed that if Susan did something similar in the future, Jill would let her supervisor know.

 NT TIP: It is imperative that your words sound genuine and convey an intention to resolve a conflict or disagreement. If you are unsure about how you sound to others, use a tape recorder to practice stating opinions and giving feedback in the right way.

Feedback and Criticism

"I don't take criticism well and I'll dig in my heels if I don't want to do something. That will frustrate anyone who tries to manage me."
Manufacturer's Representative, age 39

The previous chapter discussed how to give feedback to others. It is equally important that you are able to accept feedback that is given to you, and deal constructively with criticism.

Without feedback, you wouldn't know where your job performance is strong and where you need to make improvements. It is part of a manager's job to provide positive and negative feedback to the people who report to him or her. Most companies have a formal schedule of when managers provide feedback to employees, usually during an annual or semi-annual performance review. Managers also receive feedback, at their performance reviews and through 360-degree feedback surveys. These surveys are given to the manager's peers, superiors and subordinates (thus the name "360" or "full circle" input) who answer questions about the manager's abilities and areas for development or improvement.

Criticism is an unfavorable evaluation of a project, task or behavior. Although the terms negative feedback and criticism can be used interchangeably, I think of criticism as a concrete directive about specific behavior or performance that an individual needs to change (e.g. "There are too many errors in this report"). I think of feedback as guidance about how to enhance overall performance (e.g. "You need to prioritize better and keep people informed about project status").

I make a distinction between feedback and criticism for a reason. Clients frequently share their performance reviews with me. It is not uncommon that "difficulty accepting criticism" is noted as an area for improvement. This usually refers to specific items in need of correction, such as: listening to others, following instructions, accepting others' ideas, or checking work for errors. Often the individual challenges his or her supervisor about the criticism; denying that it is true, or trying to justify their actions. This can have negative consequences on the job.

The first thing to do if you receive criticism is to listen to what is being said and try to understand why that person needed to provide it. Do not take it as a personal affront or attack. Perhaps, you do not understand expectations or need additional training. Maybe you need to work on your communication skills or learn how to follow someone else's rules. Criticism provides you the opportunity to make the changes and be successful.

Many of my clients confuse feedback with criticism and take it very personally. As a result, they miss the real message and focus their energy on changing the wrong thing. William's performance review described two areas for improvement. He was asked to summarize the main points during presentations, instead of providing a lot of detail, and to use less technical language that everyone can understand. William, who was hoping for a promotion, thought that the review was very negative. "This is saying that I can't advance," he said. "No," I replied, "it is telling you *how* to advance." Once he could see the feedback as a roadmap for his development, we were able to focus on how William could adjust his presentations to sell his ideas to an executive audience.

Feedback describes how other people perceive you. You then have the chance to manage those perceptions by continuing to do more of what is working and changing what is not.

It may surprise you to know that you are making an impression on the people you work with every day. Even if their impressions do not represent the truth of the situation, they do represent that person's experience. This is important to know because people will react to you based on how they perceive you. For instance, an individual who is perceived as friendly but "eccentric" will be treated differently than one who is perceived as unfriendly and strange. Unless you are aware of the impression you are making on others, you cannot do anything to change it.

This is why you should listen to feedback without becoming defensive. After Jeff learned that his colleagues found him to be very critical, he changed the way that he spoke to others. His colleagues noticed the change and after a few months, came to welcome Jeff's thoughtful suggestions.

How to use criticism and feedback constructively:
- Do not interrupt and begin questioning the validity of what you are hearing or attempt to justify your point of view.

- Listen carefully and take notes. Ask questions to clarify what you don't understand.

- Think about why people perceive you as they do. Get some help with this if necessary from your work buddy or supervisor. Have people said similar things before? Can you see how the reactions of others make sense within the context of the situation?

- Figure out specific actions that you can take to change people's perceptions or address criticisms.

Dealing with Authority

"Making a list of people and their roles helps me remember the levels of respect due managers and the camaraderie due peers."

Food Service Worker and Educator, age 56

Peter came to see me because he was unhappy with his performance review. Peter felt that he had done an outstanding job over the prior year and was expecting an excellent evaluation and a raise. His supervisor saw Peter's performance differently. Peter was described a difficult to work with and unable to prioritize projects. He was also taken to task for not keeping colleagues informed about project delays.

As we went over Peter's employment history, a pattern emerged. In his previous jobs, he had experienced significant conflict with his supervisor and other senior members of the organization. Often the conflicts became serious enough that Peter was fired or chose to resign before being let go. "What am I missing?" he asked.

Difficulty dealing with authority can become a chronic problem that results in multiple job losses. As resumes grow longer, with one short-term position after another, it gets harder and harder to explain why employment lasts months instead of years, and to find a new job.

Sometimes, you wind up with an unreasonable, difficult boss. Individuals can be promoted into supervisory roles because they excel at technical aspects of their jobs, not because they are skilled at managing others. Office politics can also land people in positions of authority for which they are not ready or qualified. Supervisors can overuse their authority, have poor communication skills (yes, even NTs can have problems with communication!) or be overwhelmed by their responsibilities.

However, if it seems to you that all of your bosses are jerks, the problem is probably with you. Your supervisor does not work in a vacuum; he or she has a boss, too. There are times when managers must implement policies, even though they don't agree with them. If there is a productivity problem in your department, the supervisor is accountable and expected to fix it.

If conflict with people in authority has become an on-going problem for you, or you are concerned that it will be, the reason might be one or more of the following:

- *Believing that your boss doesn't deserve your respect because you are intellectually superior.* The problem with this attitude is that success in the neurotypical workplace usually is as dependent on soft skills (e.g. getting along with others), as raw intelligence. Your supervisor will probably sense your contempt and be even less inclined to want to work with you (and may want to fire you). Focus on cultivating skills such as treating others with respect, being cooperative and working well on a team.

- *Continually questioning or challenging assignments.* You must accept that it is your supervisor's role to direct the activities of the people reporting to him or her. Generally, the less complex the job, the more control the supervisor has over how it will be done. Even in cases where it is acceptable to question an assignment (e.g. if you have a manager level position) you must choose your battles. Differentiate between suggesting a legitimate improvement and simply wanting to do something your own way.

- *Treating your supervisor as an enemy.* Coming into work each day prepared for battle makes it almost certain that you will find one. There are clients who tell me in great detail about how unreasonable, mean and uncaring their supervisor is, despite the fact that this same supervisor has given them a promotion or raise. Just because your supervisor doesn't handle something the way that you want, it doesn't mean that they are wrong or being mean. You may be misinterpreting a situation or a person's actions, or overreacting based on your anxiety.

 NT TIP: If you are having difficulties with your boss, try to find out if other people in your department are having problems with the boss, too. Pick one or two people who you trust and raise the subject in a subtle way. You might ask, "I've been getting a lot of criticism from Mike about the time it takes me to finish the reports. Have you had this problem, too?"

- *Treating your supervisor like a peer.* Even if the standard in your work place is to address your supervisor by his or her first name, some degree of deference is expected. Observe how other people in your department, particularly your peers, interact with the supervisor. Be particularly sensitive about avoiding behaviors that could embarrass your supervisor in front of others, like pointing out an error, or that bring your loyalty into question, such as criticizing a decision.

- *Refusing to do something because you think it is dumb.* Instead of ignoring the request or bluntly stating your opinion, try to understand the reason behind it. Use language and a tone of voice that express curiosity, not condemnation. "You want me to use the copy machine at the end of the hall. I'm curious about why I can't use the one near my desk." Or, "It seems redundant for both Bill and me to review the statistics. Is there a reason that it is handled that way?" Do not question every process or it will appear that you are challenging your supervisor's authority and decision making abilities. If you are new on the job, learn the existing system first. You might come to understand reasons behind procedures that initially don't make sense to you.

CHAPTER FIVE

Executive Functions at Work

"A big challenge in every way!"

Fiber Artist, age 50

Executive functions are cognitive processes that enable a person to develop, organize and execute a plan. Good executive functioning allows an individual to analyze facts and draw conclusions, prioritize, solve problems, predict likely outcomes, evaluate results and change course if needed. He is able to synthesize data from various sources to form an understanding the big picture. He recalls similar experiences from the past, and uses them to inform his current decisions.

Despite having more than 15 years of experience as a copywriter, Mary could not estimate how long it would take her to create the various marketing brochures, advertisements, and email campaigns that were assigned to her. Although the quality of her work was very good, she had lost several jobs because she could not work fast enough to meet the required deadlines.

Peter lasted just two weeks in his part-time job as a bus boy. "My boss said that I was moving too slowly and should have found things to do when the restaurant wasn't busy. How do you know what to do, though, if no one tells you?" Now a junior in college, Peter lost a number of jobs when he was in high school as well. "I can do complex, technical jobs, but not simple ones," he said.

Martin was crushed to lose a retail job, after less than one month. Although his full-scale IQ was in the superior range, he had been unable to find work in finance. The retail job seemed like a good way to earn some cash, while he continued looking for a financial analyst position. There were problems from the start. He had a hard time remembering and following the verbal instructions he was given during the training period. He admitted that his "social judgment" was poor. He once called out, "We have an irate customer here," within ear shot of the annoyed patron. He impulsively used his supervisor's computer without permission. He was having trouble completing a transaction. Instead of calling a manager for help, he spent nearly half an hour trying to get the register to work, oblivious to the growing throng of impatient shoppers.

Many individuals with Asperger's Syndrome find that executive function problems impact their work performance. In Martin's case, poor working memory made it hard for him to remember verbal instructions. He had to compensate by writing things down. Mary had difficulty planning the sequence of steps needed to complete a project, as well as estimating the amount of time each step would take. She didn't recognize similarities among assignments, and treated each brochure as a brand new task. Getting started on something new was hard. Once she began her work, she would become stuck midway through, realizing that she had overlooked an important element that had to be completed first. Supervisors frequently told Mary that she spent too much time on non-essential tasks.

Good executive functioning also requires flexibility so that you can adjust your approach if something isn't working and identify options.

This section discusses common executive function difficulties at work and what you can do to mitigate them.

Working Memory and the Myth of Multitasking

"Multitasking [is the biggest challenge] because I will be working on something and four other people need something NOW."
Administrative Assistant, age 31

Multitasking is defined as the ability to do several things at the same time. We envision someone simultaneously replying to email, talking on the telephone and thinking about what they will say at the staff meeting which starts in 10 minutes. That is the myth. The reality is that when people multitask they are not literally doing more than one thing at once. They are rapidly shifting their attention from one task to another. Doing this requires the ability to quickly process information and having a good working memory.

Working memory refers to a small amount of information that the brain stores for immediate use. When you dial someone's telephone number or key in their email address, you are accessing working memory.

You also use working memory when you learn something new. The process of learning to drive a car is commonly used as an illustration. At first, it takes a lot of working memory capacity to consciously remember all of the steps: put key in the ignition ... start engine ... fasten seat belt ... put car into reverse ... check rear-view mirror ... step on accelerator ... etc. After much repetition, the information moves into long-term memory storage and the process of driving becomes routine. Instead of reviewing the individual steps, a person "drives to the store."

Although it is not possible to fix poor working memory, there are techniques that you can use to improve it, and expand your ability to multitask.

- Find a quiet work space and limit interruptions during the day. Depending on your job, you may be able to close your office door or post a "do not disturb" sign outside of your cubicle so that you can work uninterrupted for a period of time. If you are in the middle of an important task and a co-worker interrupts, ask if you can speak at a later time, "I am working on deadline right now; can we talk at 3:00?"

- Schedule two or three specific times per day for checking voice- and e-mails. Turn off the email notification system on your computer. Reduce auditory distractions by wearing noise-cancelling headphones or using a white noise machine.

- Do not assume that you have to start everything from scratch. Instead, look for connections to what you already know about a task or situation. If you're writing a brochure, for instance, think about brochures that you have written in the past ("I need a headline, three or four benefits to bullet-point on the cover, a sub-head for the inside...").

- If an assignment is unlike any you've done before, find an example and use that to create an outline. Then fill in the outline with specific details of your project. If you are writing a newsletter article for the first time, find examples of newsletters, either those previously published by your company, or newsletters from organizations in the same field. Notice the front page news stories that are continued inside of the publication; whether there are photographs or not; the average length of the stories; topics covered; etc.

- Practice information "chunking." The average adult can store about seven pieces of information in their working memory. Grouping pieces of information into categories uses less working memory capacity. A classic example of chunking is the telephone number. The sequence 9785553210 is difficult to remember. But when the digits are categorized into area code, prefix, and line number, recall is much easier: (978) 555-3210.

- Create daily routines, instead of relying on working memory to plan activities.

- Writing things down using a pencil or pen, not a computer keyboard, aids recall. Some of my clients carry small pads with them for this purpose.

- Make use of electronic devices to organize information, schedule appointments and remind yourself of commitments.

Project Planning

"I am always forgetting meeting times, places and subjects ... what is due and when it's due."
              Network Analyst, age 40

Planning is a critical executive function at work. Acting without a plan can have a number of consequences, such as: not knowing how to get started, becoming stuck midway through a project, vastly underestimating how long a task will take, discovering too late that important items have been omitted, or losing sight of the original goal.

  There are four basic steps to effective planning: establish a clear goal or task; create specific, manageable steps to reach the goal; estimate the time needed to complete the steps; gather/obtain the materials needed to finish the project.

The planning template on the next page has been used by my clients for both long-term projects and daily tasks. It helps you to organize specific steps and estimate the time they take to complete. If you are like many of my clients, you find the concept of time is elusive. You may not know how much can be accomplished in 15 minutes or how much time has passed when you have been working on a task.

 NT TIP: A basic technique for estimating time is make associations between a current project and similar one from the past. If you once spent 90 minutes editing 20 pages of a manuscript, it is safe to assume that it will take about the same time to edit 20 pages of an instructional manual. Factor in additional time if a task is more complex. If an instructional manual contains 20 pages of text, plus detailed diagrams, add 45 minutes to your estimate. If you are working on a new task, ask your co-workers for advice: "How much time would you allocate to do X?", "Does 2 hours seem like enough time to process all of these orders?"

The italic type on the planning template shows how one of my clients used it to plan the writing of a manual for his company's engineering group.

At first, this process can be time consuming, but it does get easier with practice. Over time, you should notice that your ability to plan is more efficient and that your projects get done on or ahead of schedule.

The Importance of Flexibility and Processing Speed in Decision Making

Brendan felt trapped in his project management job. Over the previous 16 months, his role had changed, involving much more interaction with co-workers from other departments. While his knowledge of internal processes was vast, his understanding of company politics was limited. More and more often, he would explode at co-workers who missed their deadlines or made what he considered to be

Planning Template

1. **Describe the goal or task:** *Produce a process manual*

2. **Due date:** *One month*

3. **Define steps and *estimated* time to complete:**
   - Step 1: *Outline sections*
     Estimated time: *4 hours*

   - Step 2: *Identify colleagues who will edit each section*
     Estimated time: *1 hour*

   - Step 3: *Write first draft*
     Estimated time: *40 hours (4 hours per day, 5 days per week for 2 weeks)*

   - Step 4: *Send draft to colleagues for editing*
     Estimated time: *30 minutes to send / 1 week for comments*

   - Step 5: *Incorporate feedback into final document*
     Estimated time: *2 hours*

   Total estimated time: *47½ hours plus 1 week for comments*

4. **What I need to complete the task (materials, information, equipment, etc.):** *Samples of process documents from other departments, organizational chart, meeting with supervisor to review initial outline*

5. **I will work on this project from:** *9:30-11:30am and 3:30-5:30pm on Mondays, Wednesdays and Thursdays; 11:00am-1:00pm and 4:00-6:00pm on Tuesdays and 8:30am-12:30pm on Fridays*

6. **At the half-way point, my goal is to have the following amount of work completed:** *60% of the first draft written*

7. ***Actual* time to complete:**
   - Step 1: *3½ hours*
   - Step 2: *45 minutes*
   - Step 3: *60 hours*
   - Step 4: *15 minutes / 2 weeks for all comments*
   - Step 5: *6 hours*

   Total actual time: *70½ hours and 1 extra week for comments*

8. **If the actual time to complete a step/task took longer than estimated time:**

   a. **What obstacles, if any, were not anticipated?**
   Draft took much longer due to unfamiliarity with part of the product development process; colleagues had more changes than I expected; two managers could not get feedback to me within a week due to travel schedules.

   b. **How can the task be handled differently next time?** *Allow 50% more time to write the document than I expect; check managers' travel schedules in advance; make sure that I am familiar with all aspects of the development process before beginning project.*

"stupid" mistakes. It was increasingly difficult to manage his workload or meet the expectations of other departments. He came home from work exhausted, but had trouble sleeping through the night.

After one particularly trying day, Brendan arrived for his coaching session tense and upset. I revisited a subject that we had discussed before. "Is this the right job?" I asked. He became agitated. "No!" he exclaimed, "but I can't leave. I don't interview well, so no one will hire me. And the job I really want requires a doctorate, and there is no way I can work and pursue a degree. I've tried to change careers and nothing works. The only option I have is to find a way to survive this job."

I asked him to describe the failed attempt to change careers. He related how, after being laid off, he decided to enter the life sciences field. After meeting with just one headhunter, Brendan was convinced that the only way to enter the life sciences was to get a doctorate. With his unemployment benefits about end and his cash reserves low, he found another job similar to the one he had lost.

Brendan's single, aborted attempt to change careers happened 16 years ago. It was still hard for him to conceive of how he could handle things differently today to have a better outcome. I have observed the same kind of rigid mindset among job seekers who insist that a particular company isn't hiring. "When was the last time you checked?" I'll ask. One man said, "Three years ago."

Flexibility is important for good decision making. Company policies change. New managers arrive. Technology, regulations and economic events transform industries. The more flexible your mindset is, the more easily you can adapt change and consider all of the options.

SUGGESTIONS TO INCREASE YOUR MENTAL FLEXIBILITY:

- *Get in the habit of thinking about options, instead of acting on your first impulse.* Do this when you are in a relaxed frame of mind. Options can be hard to see when you are agitated. Brainstorm with a friend to generate a larger number of possibilities. Write them all down and predict the likely outcome of each.
- *Practice grayscale thinking.* Instead of absolute terms (right or wrong; good or bad) consider both/and or if/then

scenarios. Dave thought that working full time meant that he would have no time for his favorite hobbies. He switched to grayscale thinking, "How can I do both?", and discovered that he would have plenty of time for hobbies on the weekends.

- **Use the debater's trick and argue an opposing point of view even if you strongly disagree with it.** Challenging yourself to find the merit in the opposite position helps you become more flexible and may just change your mind.

The processing speed also impacts decision making. Processing speed is the rate at which the brain takes information in from your various senses (sight, touch, hearing, etc.), organizes and interprets it, and then decides what action to take. It is usually a function of neurology, and has no correlation to a person's intelligence.

If you, like many people with AS, have slower brain processing speed, it means that you literally need time to think. My clients describe feeling "barraged" or "ambushed" when people ask them several questions in rapid succession. Unable to take in all the information, make sense of it, and formulate a reply, they freeze or become very frustrated, sometimes lashing out at others.

Slow processing speed makes the rapid attention-shifting required for multitasking and group interaction difficult. It made Cindy appear chronically unprepared to answer questions posed by executives in weekly staff meetings. Concerned about her performance, she requested a written agenda 24 hours in advance of each meeting, and that she answer the questions in writing.

There are ways to compensate for a slower processing speed:

- Ask for clarification if someone says or asks something that you don't understand

- Ask that information be repeated more slowly and/or provided in written form

- Explain your difficulty in a neutral way ("I need some time to think about what you've said. Let's talk again tomorrow," or "I'm getting confused; can we go through this slowly?")

- Request an agenda in advance of meetings, or ask one of the participants share notes with you afterwards

When Brendan and I brainstormed what his career options were, we developed the following list of options and probable outcomes:

Career Option	*Likely Outcome*
1. Do nothing…	*My current workload will not get any lighter.*
2. Quit….	*I will run out of money before I can train for a new career.*
3. Start doing research on the career I want….	*Things may have changed from 16 years ago; or I might find a related career that doesn't require a doctorate.*
4. Look for another job in my current field….	*I will be happier in a less stressful environment and can probably find a new position quickly.*

Brendan ruled out options one and two and made the decision to renew his research in the life sciences sector and to look for a new job in his current line of work.

Three Simple Time Management Tips

Peter had been assigned a special project, but could not find enough time to work on it. When I asked him how much of his work week was spent on various tasks, Peter drew a blank.

The assignment I gave Peter was to track how he was spending his time. He used a simple chart that divided the work day into 15 minute increments (9:00; 9:15; 9:30; 9:45, etc.). Every day for two weeks, he indicated on the chart what he was doing and when. For example, on Monday from 10:00 – 10:30am he was in a staff meeting; from 10:30 to 11:00am he answered emails.

After the two week period, Peter was shocked to discover that 3 to 4 hours of his week was spent answering basic procedural questions. He also realized that crafting detailed replies to emails was taking an enormous amount of time and keeping him from concentrating on priorities. He decided to make two changes. One was to direct colleagues to company manuals that would answer their procedural questions. The other was to keep his emails brief and schedule face-to-face meetings to discuss complicated issues. These two changes freed up more than 15 hours per month.

The time tracking exercise is one of the most effective things that I

Some Thoughts About Email

It can be tempting to rely on email for the majority of your workplace communication. You can take your time creating or replying to a message. You can edit and re-edit your reply. There's no need to worry about making eye contact or being caught off guard by a question you can't answer.

Unfortunately, the very things that make email attractive also make it notorious for creating misunderstandings. Innocent remarks can be perceived as threats; attempts at humor are interpreted as insults. Many business people are not good writers and much of their intended meaning can be lost by the time it reaches the recipient.

Email is not to be used for addressing sensitive or complex matters. The annals of Corporate America are filled with stories about angry or inflammatory email that got the writer fired. Sometimes, people discover that they have spent the better part of an afternoon crafting lengthy replies about subjects that can't be resolved in cyberspace. If a group is involved, the in-box can rapidly fill with dozens of missives to read and reply to, although your responses are probably out of date by the time you hit the Send button.

Email can be an effective tool for conveying basic information and answering straightforward questions. However, it is not an appropriate medium for discussing emotionally-charged or complicated issues. In these cases, make a telephone call or, better yet, arrange an in-person meeting.

have found for seeing where you need to better manage your time.

Another tip is to ask your co-workers for ideas about how to increase the pace of your work and your efficiency. They may be able to clue you in on the "unspoken rules" about which tasks are really priorities and which are not. They can also show you ways to streamline your processes or consolidate steps.

Are there personal habits that you need to change? Are you adding extra time to tasks by striving for perfection? Do you spend long periods trying to solve problems on your own instead of asking for help? Do you always start from scratch without checking if there has been prior work or information available to use?

Asking for Help is a Good Thing; Being Too Helpful Is Not

Almost all of my Asperger's clients has expressed reticence about asking for help at work. Alex presumed that since he had been hired, his employer expected him to know everything about the job, on the first day. He also admitted a tendency to "reinvent the wheel," ignoring established systems and creating his own procedure for completing a task. He further admitted that his way was almost always inefficient and very time consuming.

Sarah was afraid of appearing "dumb" and would tell people that she understood things when she really didn't. Because of this, she made many errors in her work and eventually lost her job. Ben's history of misinterpreting situations made him feel ashamed to ask for help. "I got tired of being accused of not paying attention," he sighed. Josh was confused about how to ask for assistance, and was so anxious that he would be yelled at for asking the wrong question that he spent many hours trying to figure things out for himself.

It is possible, however, to ask too many questions, which will annoy your supervisor and co-workers. Some of my clients say that anxiety drives them to ask questions that they already know how to answer. The queries serve as a means of double checking or receiving validation that they are doing a good job. Concern about doing something exactly right can also cause unnecessary queries and raise concerns about your competence.

If you are new on the job, or are being trained on a new procedure or computer system, it is expected that you will have questions. Even if you had a similar position at your previous company, the new firm will have different people, procedures and policies. This is why many organizations have formal training periods, which can last from a few days to several weeks. Or, an experienced member of the department is assigned to show a newcomer "the ropes," i.e. what needs to be done and how to do it.

Asking about what you don't understand is smart to do. Otherwise you could waste a lot of time on work that will have to be redone. No matter how long you have been with a company, asking colleagues for suggestions or advice when you face a new situation is a strategy that will enable you to find better solutions in less time. (Savvy managers "know what they don't know" and surround themselves with people who have skills or expertise they don't have.)

Determine to whom you should direct your requests for assistance. In jobs that are process oriented (e.g. data entry, accounts receivable, retail sales, etc.) this might clearly be your direct supervisor or a peer. If you are in a manager-level position or higher, the correct "who" depends on the nature of the query. The expectation usually is that you will find answers to common, procedural items on your own or through a co-worker. Matters that have the potential to significantly impact sales, profits, expenses, critical deadlines, or the work of people in other departments should involve your supervisor. If you are completely confused about where to go for an answer, ask a peer ("Who should I ask about X?").

Keep notes about who you should contact with various questions or problems so that you are not asking the same people the same thing again and again. People will be irritated if they believe that you are not paying attention.

Asking too many questions may be a sign that you do not understand a fundamental part of an assignment or task. Rather than continually interrupting your colleagues, write down everything that you are unclear about. Arrange a meeting with your supervisor, a colleague, your work buddy or human resources to review the items on your list. If you need additional training, more practice or written instructions, say so.

If colleagues consistently resist answering your questions, this could indicate a bigger problem. For instance, if you often hear, "The answer is in your training manual," or "You should know how to answer that," it is a signal that you are expected to try to find the answer on your own. If you are told, "We discussed this last week," it could show a problem with short-term memory (in which case you need to start taking notes). Or it could mean that you need to listen more carefully in the future. If you receive a response such as, "You should know that by now," it points to a need for additional training or it's a sign that people are annoyed with you.

Neurotypicals may be surprised when you ask about things that are very obvious to them. They may reply with remarks like, "That's obvious," "Common sense should tell you," or a sarcastic, "What do you *think* the answer is?!" Refuse to be intimidated by these kinds of responses. Do not become angry, because most NTs know little or nothing about Asperger's Syndrome. Instead, disarm the situation in a way that gets your question answered. One effective technique is to say, in a sincere voice, "Actually, it is not obvious to me. Would you explain what I need to do?" or "I guess I don't have common sense. Tell me what I am missing." You can also try a bit of self-deprecating humor, such as, "I can be kind of dense when it comes to figuring out what people want. Please spell it out very precisely for me." Use this kind of humor sparingly, or it will appear to people that you lack self-confidence.

Use caution and discretion if you have questions concerning social skills, basic communication and interpersonal relationships. It is inappropriate to ask your supervisor how to make small talk, whether you make enough eye contact, or why your peers don't invite you to lunch. Questions like these are best addressed by someone outside of the office, such as a coach, psychotherapist or family member. If you are confused about office politics, or the personality styles, preferences and expectations of others, ask your work buddy for guidance.

Clearly, asking for help when you need it is the smart thing to do. But what if you want to offer help and advice to others? Have you ever had the experience of trying to be supportive only to have people accuse you of being selfish or rude?

John was thrilled to get hired as a sales associate for a major retail chain. During his first week assisting customers on the sales floor, he received several compliments from his supervisor. By week two, things had begun to go downhill. John noticed what seemed to be glaring inefficiencies in the sales system, and began challenging his boss and the other associates about the procedures. "I thought they would be glad to know about a better way to do things," he said.

Nearly a month into the job, John was fired. One reason for his termination: refusal to follow company procedures. At our first coaching session, John slumped in his chair. "I was only trying to help and I got fired," he said.

Lisa was shocked to learn at her performance review that colleagues complained that she was critical, judgmental and a "nitpicker." At issue was her habit of correcting people when they made grammatical and pronunciation mistakes or deviated from a standard procedure. "I thought people would want to know when they did something wrong," she said.

Both John and Lisa thought that they were making positive contributions. What happened?

In John's case, he didn't think about the big picture. Although his suggestions might have made his job more efficient, other departments would have had to change their systems as a result. John made the mistake of suggesting changes without fully understanding why certain procedures were currently in place. Additionally, he had gone outside of his assigned job responsibilities in trying to redesign the sales processes.

Lisa's mistake concerned situational context. When she was doing her copy editing, it was appropriate that she correct grammatical errors. However, within the context of informal discussions during staff meetings, correcting others was unwelcome and perceived as arrogant.

A general rule for offering help is this: be sure that the other person wants it. Unsolicited advice and error correction are usually unwelcome. The exceptions are situations where your comments will spare someone embarrassment ("There is some mayonnaise on your chin") or prevent an accident or serious error ("You'll be cut if you hold the blade that way").

☞ **NT TIP:** It is considered rude to eavesdrop on conversations, and especially rude to eavesdrop and then point out someone's error!

Be certain that your helpfulness is not violating any company policies or rules. Brendan was reprimanded for accepting returns of video games that had been opened. The store policy was to make refunds only on products in unopened packages. Although he wanted to help the customers, his first responsibility was to follow company guidelines.

Meeting Employer Expectations

"Find a way to prioritize based on what your employer needs from you, not what you think is important."

Industrial Hygienist, age 50

The topic of job performance creates anxiety for many of the individuals I coach. Some have been stunned to receive poor performance reviews or to lose their jobs. "I thought everything was fine," they exclaim. "Why didn't anyone tell there was a problem months ago?" Their supervisors *did* tell them, but in ways that they didn't understand. Others have received feedback about areas to improve, but don't know exactly what kind of changes need to be made. They become paralyzed with confusion or anxiety and do nothing, or become so frustrated that they impulsively act on poorly reasoned ideas.

Seth's supervisor gave him two months to correct several performance problems or be fired. Seth edited a professional journal in the life sciences field. Recently his duties had expanded to include formatting articles and other production functions. Seth was finding it hard to keep up with the new demands.

Two weeks after their initial meeting, Seth met again with his supervisor, Marcia. She was confused that Seth wasn't proactively addressing his performance short falls. "She didn't think that I was trying because I didn't take her suggestions to use checklists, come to meetings prepared, and try to find answers to questions on my own," Seth sighed.

Seth found Marcia's rapid questioning about the status of his projects very stressful, "and the stress makes my brain shut down." Increasingly overwhelmed, Seth focused more and more on details of his editing, while the publication itself got farther and farther behind schedule.

Understanding expectations requires strong communication and executive function skills. Misunderstandings can happen if you interpret instructions very literally, or don't notice non-verbal signals such as an impatient stare or annoyed tone of voice. Neurotypicals are big picture thinkers and assume that details are implicitly understood. They will not explain what the fine points are unless asked. It is up to you to clarify tasks and assignments:

- Ask for a review or for written instructions if you have forgotten the steps in a procedure.
- Request a sample or submit an outline if instructions are vague or you are uncertain what the finished product should look like ("Can you show me an example of what you want?").
- Ask for assistance if you are unsure of how to get started ("Can we walk through this project?").
- Summarize your understanding of an assignment, "You want me to update the ledger first and then start processing the

checks." Summarize using your own words; do not repeat what the other person said verbatim.

- Ask your manager how often he or she wants to be updated on project status, how you should handle questions, and, if applicable, what decisions you can make.

- Observe your peers to understand "unspoken" expectations. Anna noticed that when there were few customers in the retail store, her fellow sales associates would take unsold clothing from the dressing rooms and return it to racks on the sales floor.

Another way to gauge how well you are meeting expectations is to ask for feedback about your performance at regular intervals. The frequency depends on your job and length of employment. If you are newly hired, requesting feedback from your supervisor after two or four weeks of employment is appropriate. If you are a manager, ask for a one-month review. Asking for feedback too often makes you appear uncertain and insecure about how to do your job.

Frame your request in a positive manner, for example, "I want to be sure that I'm meeting your expectations. Can we set up a meeting next week to discuss my performance?" If the first session goes well, it may not be necessary to schedule another meeting until your regular performance review. If your supervisor recommends areas for you to improve, ask when he or she would like to have a follow up meeting to assess your progress.

Requesting performance feedback is not the same as asking questions about specific tasks or assignments. If an assignment isn't clear, ask, don't guess what to do.

If you, like Seth, are experiencing on-going problems meeting your supervisor's expectations, then other strategies are in order. A technique that I have used to help my clients be more proactive in addressing performance issues has three steps.

First, define the specific problem that you want to address. Second, describe the end result that you want. Third, brainstorm possible solutions and predict the likely outcomes of each solution. If you are having difficulty developing solutions, find a friend or co-worker to help you.

When Seth tried this technique, he was surprised at the number of different solutions that he was able to find. He defined one problem as: Marcia says that I ask her too many detailed questions about the production process for the journal. She expects that I will find the answers to 80% of these questions on my own.

Seth defined the result that he wanted as follows: When I am able to answer most of these questions myself, Marcia will see that I am listening to her and making changes.

Next he brainstormed possible solutions and predicted what the likely outcomes would be:

Possible Solution	*Likely Outcome*
1. Keep asking Marcia questions; she is my boss and it is her job to answer them…	Marcia will continue to be frustrated with me and think that I cannot do the job.
2. Write down my questions as they come up during the day. After 4:00, review them one by one….	I won't be as stressed and will probably remember where to find at least some of the answers.
3. Create a list of the most frequent questions that I have and where I can find the answers….	This will be a quick, easy way to remember the resources that are available to me.

Seth selected solutions two and three and began implementing them. Within two weeks, Marcia commented about his being proactive and that she had seen improvements in his work.

Like Seth, you may find that this process is time consuming at first. However, the solutions that you identify will serve as templates which can be applied again and again in similar situations.

A variation on this exercise is to think about what kind of impression that you want to make on others. Tina had been told by prior managers that colleagues found her rude and difficult to work with. She was fired from two jobs because of her poor interpersonal relationships.

It had never occurred to Tina that people formed opinions of her based on her behavior, or that she could manage those opinions. She and I began by defining the specific problem: People think that I am rude because I snap at them or yell when I am stressed. Next, Tina described her desired result: I want people to perceive me as friendly and cooperative. We brainstormed and came up with these solutions:

Possible Solution	Likely Outcome
1. Stop talking to people altogether…	I will be seen as even more unfriendly; this solution is unrealistic because I have to talk to people to get my work done.
2. Join co-workers for lunch once per week….	People will see that I am making an effort; it might be awkward because I am not sure of what to say.
3. Find ways to manage stress at work…	Instead of yelling I will focus on answering questions calmly.
4. Observe how my peers interact and make a list of behaviors that demonstrate friendliness….	People will like me better and want to work with me.
5. Watch the evening news so that I am better informed and can more easily join in small talk….	This will show people that I want to interact with them.

Although Tina liked the idea of joining her co-workers for lunch, she was very anxious about how to act. We decided to concentrate on solutions three and four first, breaking them down into small steps.

 NT TIP: If you are having repeated problems meeting expectations, ask yourself whether you are in the right job. Are you in a position that emphasizes your challenges instead of maximizing your strengths? Do you find yourself regularly redoing assignments, missing deadlines or working significantly longer hours than your peers? If so, find an advisor who can help you determine whether you need additional skills or should explore other lines of work.

Understand Your Learning Style

Learning style refers to the methods by which an individual learns best. There are three categories of learning style: visual, auditory and tactile/kinesthetic. Most people have a clear preference for one category, although some prefer a combination of two or all three styles.

It may be possible to change the way that you are given assignments to match they way that you prefer to learn. I have had clients who made accommodation requests based on their preferred method of processing information. An example of this is asking for written materials instead of verbal instructions.

There are many free online tests that can help you determine your learning style. One of my favorites is at www.LdPride.net.

- **Visual learners** want to see information in words, diagrams or pictures. They prefer detailed notes and written outlines, along with charts, photos and diagrams. Color-coding and the use of visual reminders, like sticky notes and icons, are useful aids for organizing work and remembering tasks.
- **Auditory learners** prefer to hear information. They learn best by attending lectures, participating in group discussions, and listening to spoken and recorded instructions. Auditory learners often talk themselves through a process or procedure.
- **Tactile/kinesthetic learners** are literally "hands-on." They enjoy participating in demonstrations, making models or learning while doing, such as operating a new piece of machinery. One technique tactile learners can use for remembering sequential information is to write each step on separate index cards, and then arrange the cards into the correct sequence.

An auditory/visual learner might listen to instructions first and then refer to written text. A visual/tactile learner might read about a procedure and then try the steps himself. Experiment to discover which methods work best for you.

The Importance of a Goal and a Plan

Whether you want to find the right career, get a new job, improve your on-the-job performance or advance in your career, it is important to start with a clear goal. This may sound obvious, but many of my clients set goals for themselves that are too vague, too general or difficult to act upon. For example, "get along better with others," or "find a job that I'll like."

It is difficult to develop an effective plan if the specific outcome that is desired is not clearly defined. Many individuals have success using the SMART goals template because it focuses them on the explicit results that they want.

SMART is an acronym that stands for **S**pecific, **M**easurable, **A**chievable, **R**easonable and **T**ime-oriented. There are five steps to creating a SMART goal. Seth, who was mentioned in the previous section on meeting employer expectations, used these five steps to address production problems with his journal.

Step 1: Make the goal Specific. Seth took a general goal, "avoid production problems," and made it very clear. The new goal: *Produce editions of the journal on time and without errors beginning with fall issue.*

Step 2: Make success Measurable. In other words, define how you will know when you've achieved your goal. Seth's measurement of success is: *Issues will be laid out correctly the first time and I will avoid having to fix mistakes at the last minute.*

Step 3: Select a goal that you can Achieve. Evaluate whether you have the skills, ability and resources needed to meet your objective. Seth's goal is achievable because he has developed a detailed check list of the sequential steps in the production process.

Sometimes people discover that their goal is not achievable. If this happens, do not get discouraged. It may be that you need to complete one or two intermediate steps first. Mike, for example, wants a job in Web development but his poor interviewing skills prevent employers from understanding his capabilities. His ultimate goal of a Web development job is not achievable until he learns how to interview well.

Perhaps you need to modify your goal based on new information.

Once Jane realized she would have a hard time with the amount of people contact required for front desk work at a public library, she changed her goal to becoming an archivist.

Step 4: Check that your goal is Reasonable. Setting a goal that isn't realistic results in frustration and wasted energy. Unrealistic goals that some of my clients have set: seeking a management-level job with no prior work experience; pursuing a career in meeting planning when the individual can't keep track of their own appointments; applying for technical positions, expecting that an employer will provide on the job training on basic software applications.

Seth confirmed that his goal is reasonable. He understands the production process and also that he cannot rely on his memory to get everything done. Using a checklist is a realistic solution to assure that each step is completed.

Step #5: Make the goal Time-oriented. Set a reasonable date to achieve your goal. This allows you to work backwards to create a timeline for each action step. Seth created a timeline with specific deadlines for completing his checklist, and each phase of the production cycle.

Once you have determined what your SMART goals are, you are ready to create a step-by-step action plan for achieving them.

CREATING AN ACTION PLAN THAT WORKS

Setting a goal is easy. The follow through needed to reach the goal is harder. If you are having trouble implementing a plan, these common "action inhibitors" may be getting in your way:

- Unsure of how to begin or what the specific steps are
- Anxiety or fear about a particular step (e.g. afraid of making phone calls)
- Boredom with tasks
- Negative attitude; paralyzed by thoughts such as, "It won't work anyway, so why bother?"
- Bad habits consume the time needed to work on a goal (e.g. hours of non-job-related Internet surfing)

- No structure to the day or week (although it sounds counter-intuitive, too much unstructured time can make it hard to get things done!)
- Trying to make a change with little or no support
- Action items are too large, not specific enough, or overwhelming (e.g. "develop a network" vs. "email one former co-worker")

A good action plan establishes the specific steps you will take, and when, to reach your goal. It is imperative that your plan is realistic. Luke was exploring careers and wanted to set up informational interviews. I asked him to create a schedule for when he would research companies and make contacts. He came to the next coaching session with a plan for 8 hours of research per day. Clearly not realistic and guaranteed to fail!

Your chance of success is higher if your goal is meaningful and important to you. The action steps must be detailed and have specific milestones. I check with my clients to make sure that they are not feeling anxious or overwhelmed with creating or following through on their weekly action plans. If they are, then they need to make revisions.

Another successful technique is to make yourself accountable to another person. Whether this is a coach, mentor, counselor, family member or friend, you should arrange regular, frequent check-ins to monitor your progress. Tell this person beforehand what he or she should do if you do not follow through with your commitments.

If you take an action and it doesn't work, brainstorm a different approach. Too often, people allow one or two setbacks to completely stop their progress. The most successful clients are the ones who take small, consistent steps over a reasonable period of time and who are willing to experiment with new techniques.

This action plan that was created by James. He was unhappy with his current job and wanted to find a similar position with a different company. James worried that his skills were out of date, and that he would not be able to make as much money at another firm.

Action Item: Research the salary range and skill requirements for senior software programmers.

Steps:

- Search online job boards for open positions
  Create spreadsheet of requirements (programming languages, types of projects, years of experience)
- Find online groups for programmers and join one or two
  See if salary is addressed on message boards
- Find the date of the programmer's association meeting
  Inquire about whether one has to be a member to attend
- Create a profile on LinkedIn
  Invite at least 3 colleagues to connect during the next week
- Research trade journals
  Cost of subscription
- Visit at least two salary-survey Web sites

Notice how this format breaks a large goal into very manageable, smaller steps. James set aside 45 minutes during two evenings each week for his job research. As he worked through each item, he realized that he had been making a lot of guesses and assumptions that weren't true. He discovered that he would not need to spend thousands of dollars updating his skills as he had initially assumed. His fears about having to take a pay cut were also unjustified. Within three months, James was actively interviewing.

Some of my clients use rewards to motivate themselves after the initial rush of motivation starts to fade. A reward does not have to involve spending money. My clients have "earned" bicycle rides, time for Internet surfing, permission to sleep late on a Sunday morning, and a trip to the library to attend a free lecture.

CHAPTER SIX:

Workplace Disclosure

"Accommodations made a huge different in how I cope and perform at work."
Network Analyst, age 40

Clients often ask my opinion about whether they should disclose their Asperger's Syndrome to an employer. My reply is, "It depends." Disclosure is a personal decision. Whether it is the right option for you depends on the nature of your job, your overall performance, specific challenges that you face, whether you have had a disciplinary action, and your comfort level with disclosing a disability.

There are benefits and risks. On the plus side, disclosure provides you protections under the Americans with Disabilities Act (ADA). The ADA prohibits discrimination against people with disabilities. Some of my clients have saved their jobs by disclosing and requesting accommodations. The risk is a job offer rescinded, a promotion denied or a job lost, without the real reasons being stated. It can be difficult, expensive and time consuming to prove discrimination.

The ADA states that an employer must provide equal opportunities to qualified individuals in hiring, firing, promotions, compensation, training and development, benefits and other employment practices. A qualified individual is someone who meets the employer's job specifications for education, skills, experience and work performance.

The ADA does not contain a list of specific disabilities. Instead "disability" is broadly defined as a physical or mental impairment "that substantially limits one or more major life activities" which can include "walking, seeing, speaking, breathing, learning, performing manual tasks, caring for oneself and working [etc.]."[1] Depending on the nature

---

[1] *Job Accommodation Network*, www.askjan.org.

of an individual's impairments, he may or may not be considered disabled under the ADA.

The Americans with Disabilities Amendments Act of 2008 (ADAAA), which went into effect on January 1, 2009, significantly changes the way that disability is defined. The threshold of "substantially limits" has been lowered, and mitigating measures (e.g. medications to control symptoms) are no longer used to determine if a person has a substantially limiting impairment. Thus the ADAAA increases the number of people who qualify as disabled. It also shifts the focus from whether an employee is disabled to whether the employer meets its obligation to reasonably accommodate a disabled individual. At the time that this book was written, specific regulations for the ADAAA were still being developed.

It is beyond the scope of this book to fully describe the ADA or ADAAA. The following information is designed to give you an overview of the ADA for the purpose of helping you determine whether to disclose. The information is general, not comprehensive, and is not legal advice. Readers in the U.S. are encouraged to visit the Web site of the Job Accommodation Network (JAN, www.askjan.org) for a detailed discussion of anti-discrimination laws. JAN is a service of the U.S. Department of Labor's Office of Disability Employment Policy, and provides free information and consultations. If you believe you have experienced job discrimination, consult an employment law attorney.

Employers are compelled under the ADA to make reasonable accommodations for qualified individuals with disabilities. A qualified individual is one who meets the employer's standards for performance and productivity. An accommodation is a modification or adjustment that allows individuals to participate in the interviewing process or to perform the essential functions of their job. The modifications must be realistic and cannot cause an undue hardship for the employer.

Whether an accommodation is reasonable or not depends on your job and your company. For Susan, a data entry clerk, requesting written instructions was reasonable. Ken, however, worked as a financial analyst. His supervisor explained that Ken's job required judgment. It was not possible to provide written instructions about how to address every situation. Similarly, what is considered an undue hardship at a company with 25 employees might not be considered an undue hardship at a company with 10,000 employees.

Employers are prohibited from asking questions about medical condition or a disability on employment applications and during job interviews. After an offer of employment is made, an employer can ask medical and disability-related questions as long as they do this to everyone who is offered the same kind of job. Once you start work, an employer cannot ask disability related questions unless they are related to your job or are necessary in order for the employer to conduct business. Suppose your supervisor notices that you seem dizzy when you stand up. Your job requires you to operate machinery. In this case, the employer has a reasonable belief that you have a disability or medical condition that could pose a risk to your safety and that of others and can ask questions about your health.

You are under no legal obligation to disclose a disability, and doing so does not guarantee that you will receive a job offer or continue in your current employment. Employers do not have to lower their standards of quality or productivity for an employee who is disabled. Let's suppose that all customer service employees are expected to enter at least 30 orders per hour. Because of Asperger's Syndrome, your processing speed is slower; you can only enter 22 orders per hour. You are considered unqualified for the job.

Additionally, you must be able to perform the essential functions of your job, or you can be fired. Essential job functions are the core tasks and responsibilities for which you are hired. For an accountant, using standard accounting software would be considered an essential function. If you have visual-spatial problems that make it impossible for you to use spreadsheets, you would be considered unqualified for the position. However if you are a copywriter, entering budget information into spreadsheets once or twice a year may not be an essential function of your job. You can request an accommodation that tasks involving spreadsheets be reassigned to someone else.

Employers do not have to accommodate employees who pose a direct threat to the health or safety of themselves or others, or those who engage in serious misconduct. Losing your temper at work can be considered a direct threat. Jack's work situation deteriorated over several months. He would frequently storm out of department meetings, muttering under his breath about procedures he didn't like. He exploded at one meeting, yelling at his co-workers about his Asperger's Syndrome and why it made it hard for him to interact with others. When his boss denied Jack's request to use vacation time, Jack sent him a threatening email. He was promptly fired.

If you disclose, your employer can request proof of your diagnosis from a qualified medical professional and information about how, specifically, your disability impacts your job performance. Your employer will probably give you a form for your medical provider to fill out. You can, and should, control what information is given to your employer. It is not necessary, or desirable, to submit your full neuropsychological evaluation, or your entire medical history. Ask your medical provider to confine their comments to those items that affect your ability to perform your current job.

It's possible to ask for modifications without disclosing Asperger's Syndrome. If you have needs that can be easily met, a general request may solve the problem. You can say, for example, "I'm hyper-sensitive to office noise and I need to wear headphones to help me concentrate," or "I need written instructions; please slow down while I make notes."

The ADA does not contain a list of specific accommodations. Instead, they are decided on an individual basis. Most employers are very willing to make adjustments that are reasonable; however the discussion is a negotiation. The more prepared you are, the better your chances of getting the accommodations that you need. Here are examples of workplace accommodations that my clients have asked for and been granted:

- Use of laptop for note-taking during meetings
- Meeting notes taken by colleague
- Weekly meetings to clarify expectations, identify priorities

- Written instructions
- Lobby television turned off during shift
- Non-essential scheduling tasks reassigned to co-worker
- Permission to take breaks when overly stressed
- Staff requests submitted in writing
- Switch to a technical job instead of management role
- Move to quiet workspace
- Use of headphones

How to Disclose in a Solution-Focused Way

If you disclose, it is important that you do so in a solution-focused way. Your manager and human resources representative may know little or nothing about Asperger's Syndrome. Making a general statement such as, "I have AS and can't multitask" puts the burden of figuring out an accommodation on the people who know the least about what you need. Proactively suggesting solutions greatly increases the likelihood that your employer will implement them.

I have developed a three-step process to help my clients develop a disclosure strategy. First, determine what to disclose; second, decide how to disclose; and third, choose when to disclose.

Step 1: What to disclose. Begin by listing all of the challenges that you are facing in the interviewing process or on the job. List only the challenges that are work related. Do not include personal problems such as exhaustion when you come home from work, not having a social life, troubled relationships, etc. Describe the impact of each challenge on your current employment situation. Write down what accommodations you believe will address the challenges.

Challenge	*Impact*	*Accommodation*
Prioritizing projects	Too much time spent on non-essential tasks; misses important deadlines	Daily review with supervisor
Slow processing speed	Hard to follow group meetings and to quickly formulate replies to questions	Receive meeting agenda 24 hours in advance; submit written answers to questions

Step 2: How to disclose. Your disclosure statement should be short, simple and to the point. Include your human resources manager in addition to your supervisor so that the disclosure is officially on the record. Summarize your situation, state your challenges and explain how you believe that your requested accommodations will address them. Do not launch into a long explanation of the history of Asperger's Syndrome, theories about its cause, or all of the potential effects.

When Andy disclosed he explained, "I have a neurobiological condition called Asperger's Syndrome that makes it hard for me to multitask and remember verbal instructions. I need a quiet workspace where I won't be interrupted and written instructions for procedures."

It can be helpful to offer your supervisor and human resources representative a brief article about AS. There is an Asperger's Syndrome Guide for Employers in the Appendix of this book that explains how AS commonly affects individuals at work. Readers may photocopy the Guide for the purpose of educating their employer. When you disclose, mention the things that are going well on the job, and state your commitment to excellent performance.

It is preferable to have a discussion when you disclose. If you are absolutely unable to explain your situation verbally, you can do so with a written letter. It is prudent to follow up verbal disclosure with a written document. It should summarize what was discussed in your meeting and what everyone agreed will happen next.

Disclosing to your supervisor and human resources representative does not give them permission to tell other people in the company about your diagnosis. You control who has access to this information. If you want it kept confidential, state this clearly. If there are other people in the company whom you want to know about your AS, state specifically who those individuals are. Check that disclosure information is kept in a separate file from your general personnel records. That way, if you leave your current employer for any reason, the information will not follow you to another company.

Step 3: When to disclose. Timing is another aspect of a disclosure strategy. There are pros and cons to disclosing at various stages of the employment cycle. There are no hard and fast rules about when to disclose. What follows are some general guidelines to consider.

Should you disclose…

IN YOUR COVER LETTER OR WHEN SUBMITTING AN APPLICATION

- Yes, if your disability gives you a distinct advantage (for example, if you are applying for a job at Specialisterne)
- Yes, if you require assistance submitting an application or with the interview process
- No, if you don't have to because it may raise concerns and land your resume in the "no" pile

AT A JOB INTERVIEW

- Yes, if your challenges are so noticeable that not offering an explanation will disqualify you
- Yes, if you have concerns about your ability to meet performance expectations as this will prevent problems if you get the job
- No, if you don't have to, because it focuses attention on potential workplace problems before you have the opportunity to demonstrate how you can contribute to the company's success

WHEN YOU RECEIVE A JOB OFFER

- Yes, if you will need accommodations right away, and want to avoid any surprises after you are hired
- No, if you believe that you can meet the performance expectations, because there is a risk that an offer can be rescinded without the employer revealing why

AFTER YOU HAVE BEEN HIRED

- Yes, if your projects are consistently late or you are frequently re-doing assignments
- Yes, if you receive feedback about the same performance or interpersonal problem three times or more
- Yes, if you are thoroughly confused about expectations or cannot perform an aspect of the job

Checklist of Common Workplace Challenges

The following checklist includes common workplace challenges faced by individuals with Asperger's Syndrome. Begin by checking all of the items that you have difficulty with at work. Then decide which of those items you need to disclose to your employer.

I. COMMUNICATION CHALLENGES

- ☐ Taking instructions literally and missing implied meanings
- ☐ Unintentionally offending others with statements that are too blunt, direct or are inappropriate
- ☐ Difficulty making adequate eye contact
- ☐ Speaking too rapidly, loudly or softly
- ☐ Difficulty interacting with co-workers
- ☐ Appearing disinterested or unfriendly
- ☐ Frequently interrupting others
- ☐ Difficulty interpreting facial expressions and body language of others
- ☐ Difficulty with one's own facial expressions and body language (e.g. forgetting to smile; people say you look angry, sad, or confused when you are not)
- ☐ Other communication challenges: _____

II. EXECUTIVE FUNCTION CHALLENGES

- ☐ Taking instructions literally and missing implied meanings
- ☐ Having trouble getting started on assignments
- ☐ Not knowing how long an assignment will/should take
- ☐ Focusing too much on details
- ☐ Thinking rigidly and failing to see options
- ☐ Difficulty with short-term memory
- ☐ Working too slowly
- ☐ Not remembering verbal instructions
- ☐ Unsure of how to prioritize projects
- ☐ Being overwhelmed by interruptions
- ☐ Unsure of what needs to be done
- ☐ Appearing not to take initiative because next steps are not clear
- ☐ Asking too many questions
- ☐ Acting impulsively, based on too little information
- ☐ Resisting change
- ☐ Insisting on doing tasks your own way
- ☐ Other executive function challenges: _____

> ### CHECKLIST OF COMMON WORKPLACE CHALLENGES (CONT.)
>
> **III. SENSORY/PROCESSING/ MOTOR CHALLENGES**
>
> ☐ Visual sensitivity (to what: _____)
>
> ☐ Auditory sensitivity: hyper- or hypo- (explain: _____)
>
> ☐ Olfactory sensitivity: hyper- or hypo- (explain: _____)
>
> ☐ Tactile sensitivity (explain: _____)
>
> ☐ Group interaction difficulties due to auditory processing problems or slow processing speed
>
> ☐ Fine motor problems (difficulty writing, stuffing envelopes)
>
> ☐ Gross motor problems (difficulty walking, running, coordinating movements)
>
> ☐ Other sensory/processing/motor challenges: _____
>
> **IV. EMOTIONAL CHALLENGES**
>
> ☐ Difficulty controlling anger or frustration
>
> ☐ Exploding when asked too many questions at once
>
> ☐ Walking out of meetings when overwhelmed or upset
>
> ☐ Crying in your work area instead of going to a private space
>
> ☐ Highly anxious
>
> ☐ Difficulty accepting criticism
>
> ☐ Other emotional challenges: _____

- Yes, if you are put on a Performance Improvement Plan (PIP)
- Yes, if you receive a disciplinary action
- Yes, if you are put on a two-week notice to improve
- No, if you are meeting expectations or can address your needs with general requests
- No, in a moment of panic because you made a mistake, had a conflict with someone or are confused about an assignment

Examples of Disclosure Strategies

The following examples illustrate different disclosure strategies used by my coaching clients. They underscore the importance of a "custom-crafted" approach that addresses abilities, experience and the demands of the job.

Ann disclosed her Asperger's Syndrome in the cover letter that she submitted with her resume. She had been referred to the hiring manager by one of her mother's friends. (Hiring manager refers to the person who will be your supervisor. It is a descriptive term, not a job title.) With Ann's permission, the friend mentioned to the hiring manager that Ann has Asperger's Syndrome. In her cover letter, Ann referred briefly to her disability, putting it in a positive light. The letter read in part, "Please be assured that my disability will not interfere with my ability to do this job, and in some ways will actually be an asset. I am very reliable and on-task, and am driven to do an extremely good job. I urge you to speak with my former supervisor…"

During the interview, Ann addressed her difficulties with making eye contact and remembering to smile by saying, "I don't show a lot of emotion because of the Asperger's Syndrome. However I am very enthusiastic about this position and brought a summary of successful projects to discuss." Having this summary helped Ann recall specific achievements in her past positions. She was hired on a 3-month trial basis.

Dan's technical skills are outstanding, but he has a long history of job losses and wanted to try a new approach after his latest termination. He identified his problem areas and accommodation needs. Then, after receiving a verbal job offer (but before signing an employment agreement) Dan told his would-be manager that he has Asperger's Syndrome. He described how Asperger's affects his ability to understand body language and how he can sometimes appear rude to people. He mentioned that he would need help with prioritizing and estimating how long a project should take to complete. He was offered the job and accepted it.

For nearly 10 years, Cindy was a successful sales manager at a high-end vacation community. Despite her Asperger's Syndrome she did well working one-on-one with clients and training junior sales people. Her group often ranked number one or number two in quarterly sales.

After the company was acquired by a much larger firm, Cindy's job became less structured and she began receiving conflicting instructions from various executives in the organization. The new regional vice president said that Cindy asked too many questions and gave too much detail in her presentations. At weekly team meetings, Cindy appeared chronically unprepared to answer questions from senior executives.

Concerned about her performance, Cindy decided to disclose her Asperger's Syndrome to her supervisor and human resources representative. Her accommodation requests included receiving a written agenda one day in advance of the team meetings. She asked that managers submit their questions to her in writing and give her 24 hours to respond. These accommodations addressed auditory processing problems that made it hard for her to hear in group settings. They also mitigated her slow processing speed, which made it impossible to respond immediately to questions from managers. After implementing the changes, she was able to participate in the meetings and provide the strategic responses the management team wanted.

Cindy also requested an extra week or two to learn new processes. Her supervisor began giving her written directions, specific examples and more of his time to answer her detailed questions. Instead of telling Cindy something vague like, "take the numbers and run with it," her supervisor states specifically, "Write a 10-minute presentation based on the sales reports that will explain 3 areas where we can increase revenue."

Tina is a receptionist for a large financial firm. One of her duties is to make sure that visitors have the proper security clearance before leaving the lobby area and entering the facility. One particularly busy day, Tina issued a visitor badge to someone she thought she recognized as he rushed through the checkpoint and quickly flashed an ID. Concerned about the possible security breach, Tina reported the incident to her supervisor, who issued Tina a written warning.

Tina explained to human resources that Asperger's Syndrome affects her short-term memory and her ability to recognize faces under stress. Her employer agreed to turn off the television in the lobby during Tina's shift, because the sound is distracting to her. Employees have been instructed to send written, not verbal, visitor requests to Tina in advance so that she will have more time to process them. Signs are now posted in the lobby informing visitors that they must check in with the receptionist and show appropriate identification.

Todd contacted me as he was having an employment crisis. Employed in a director-level job for two years, his literal interpretation of instructions and difficulty seeing the big picture were frustrating his colleagues. Todd's supervisor expected him to assume "a leadership role," a general directive that was completely bewildering to Todd. When we met Todd, had been given two weeks to improve his performance or be fired.

Todd disclosed his Asperger's Syndrome and, over the next three months, Todd, his manager and a human resources representative worked out accommodations and set clear performance expectations. Then an opportunity arose for Todd (at his own request) to give up his director's position and become a senior manager instead. The new position allows Todd to use his considerable technical ability and off-load the troublesome "leadership" and people management duties. By acknowledging his strengths and limitations, and being willing to make changes, Todd went from about-to-be-fired to once again being a valuable member of his company. (He didn't have to take a pay cut, either.)

A final example is that of Adam, an extremely bright program manager at a major, international conglomerate. He is consistently praised for his extensive knowledge of supply chain management and his organization's systems. Like many people with Asperger's Syndrome, Adam is a perfectionist and can be impatient with those who don't share his knowledge and very high performance standards. Easily frustrated, he regularly engages in heated debates about minute points.

Eager for a promotion, Adam was upset to learn at his performance review that his acerbic communication style and detail focus had raised doubts about his ability to work with other departments and to think strategically. He was denied a promotion and began coaching to learn how to give feedback without alienating his colleagues. He still struggles to grasp inter-department politics and interact at a strategic level with vice presidents. At issue is whether he can negotiate the communication and executive function demands of a director-level job. He has elected not to disclose to his employer.

Sometimes, despite disclosing and giving your best efforts, you lose your job. If this happens, or has happened, to you, treat it as a learning experience. Try to find out from the employer specifically what went wrong and what you need to improve. Research other industries or professions where you can transfer your skills. Do not become discouraged. With determination and practice virtually everyone can learn new skills, gain insight into strengths and limitations and improve their personal presentation, all of which increase the odds of finding satisfying employment. (See more in Chapter 7, What to Do If You Are Fired.)

CHAPTER SEVEN

Managing Anxiety, Frustration, Anger and Stress

"I have no concept of 'checking in' or recognizing my own emotions ... and therefore may keep going until anxiety, anger or stress has built up significantly."

Inventory Control Specialist, age 32

Throughout this book, we have discussed the importance of managing how other people perceive you. Communication skills play a large role creating a positive impression, as do executive functions like flexibility, seeing the big picture, planning and prioritizing. A third factor is your ability to manage stress and emotions, such as anger, frustration, anxiety and fear. For many people with Asperger's Syndrome, just being able to recognize emotions before they become completely overwhelming is a challenge.

John became so frustrated with a co-worker that he "lost it," and quit his job on the spot. Elizabeth was so anxious about a missed deadline that she exploded at a colleague for calling her "Beth." Ellen abruptly walked out of a department meeting because she could not follow the rapid pace of the discussion. Bill began cursing when his boss wouldn't stop "barraging" him with questions about a troubled project ... and was promptly fired for insubordination.

Emotional overwhelm can lead to impulsive actions and poor decision making. There is a biological reason for this, which Daniel Goleman describes in his book *Working with Emotional Intelligence*, as an "amygdala hijack." Strong emotions like anxiety, fear and anger activate the body's fight or flight response. This in turn triggers the amygdala, or emotional part of the brain, to react. This reaction is automatic, visceral and occurs before the cerebral cortex (the thinking part of the brain) can intercede. During such episodes, an individual is literally not thinking straight. When the emotional storm passes and the thinking brain takes over once again, the person realizes that his emotional reactions were inappropriate.

With great effort, John was able to convince his employer to rehire him, but the incident has negatively impacted his decade long career with the company. "My role has been reduced," he explained, "and I am not invited to the strategy meetings anymore."

If you are unable to control the levels of stress in your life you are at risk of damaging your reputation, credibility and possible losing your job. Most companies today have "zero tolerance" policies for behaviors that are considered threatening or harassing.

If you have serious difficulties controlling your emotional reactions, get help from a psychotherapist or other medical professional. Otherwise develop a plan for coping with frustrations at work in a rational way.

In planning how to deal with strong emotions, the first step is to become aware of what triggers your anger, frustration, anxiety, panic or other feelings. I ask my clients to write down the triggers they

---

BEHAVIORS THAT WILL DAMAGE YOUR CREDIBILITY AT WORK (AND POSSIBLY GET YOU FIRED)

- Abruptly walking out of meetings
- Losing your temper
- Cursing
- Slamming your hand on a desk or wall
- Throwing objects
- Crying frequently or hysterically
- Withdrawing and refusing to answer questions
- Making accusations of being "tortured," "persecuted," "hated by everyone," etc.
- Muttering under your breath
- Threatening (verbal, written or physical) others or company property

have experience over a one- or two-week period. Together we look for patterns and figure out how to interrupt the automatic reactions to people or events.

Erin exploded when frequent interruptions by co-workers frustrated her. When she needs uninterrupted work time, she now forwards all calls directly to voice mail and hangs a Do Not Disturb sign across the entrance to her cubicle. Josh realized that his irritation in the late afternoon was triggered by not eating lunch. He no longer skips the mid-day meal.

Learn the various signals that your body sends as your stress levels rise. You can create a simple "emotional thermometer" by drawing a rating scale with designations: "calm," "mild annoyance," "moderate annoyance," "severe annoyance" and "explosion." Write down your stress signals at each stage. "Moderate annoyance" might mean that you feel your shoulder muscles tense, your breathing gets faster and your face flushes.

John's co-workers complained that when they asked him questions, he responded with anger. John began using the emotional thermometer, and identified his trigger as a situation where he felt pressured to come up with an immediate response to complex questions. Fatigue and stress made him even more impatient and irritated. He became aware of his clenched fist, increased heart rate, and the knot that formed in his stomach when his emotional temperature reached severe annoyance.

John changed how he interacts with colleagues. Instead of feeling pressured to process and reply to a question right away, he writes it down and says, "Let me think about your question and get back to you." Whenever possible he avoids meeting with people after 4:00pm, when he is tired, and when he first arrives in the morning and is eager to check email.

There are a number of things that you can do to "short-circuit" a rising emotional current:

- **Take a break.** Leaving your desk to get a drink of water, walking around the parking lot or listening to some music on your iPod can restore calm and rational thinking.

- **Do not respond to others or make decisions when you are upset.** Excuse yourself from the situation by saying, "I need some time to think; let's talk again tomorrow," or "I'm upset right now and want to calm down before discussing this further."

- **Use positive self-talk.** Repeating soothing statements silently to yourself will ease tension: "I can handle this situation," or "If I approach the problem calmly, the answer will come to me."

- **Exercise regularly.** This is a proven stress reliever that also improves your overall health.

- **Get enough sleep.** Time after time clients have reported improved mood and increased patience after getting a good night's rest.

- **Release unrealistic expectations.** Stop striving for perfection and accept that things will not always be done in the way that you would like.

How to Avoid Cognitive Distortions

Would you like to know the secret to significantly reducing your levels of frustration and improving your working relationships?

Accept that you cannot control the actions of other people. Let me repeat that. *You cannot control the actions of other people.*

It is a given that you will encounter people who annoy, frustrate or otherwise provoke you at work. People's actions are motivated by their own values, preferences and goals. It is not possible to control what other people do. All that you can control is your own reaction. And you do have choices in how you respond.

My clients frequently take the actions of other people very personally. Their assumption is that another person's words or behaviors are intended as an attack or put down. On closer examination, we see that my client is focused on one or two details and has not put the situation into the proper context. Similarly, if theory of mind skills are not strong, it can be very difficult to interpret another person's motives.

On Tim's first day at a new job, his supervisor came to his workstation to begin training him on how to use one of the company's systems. Tim turned on the computer and waited for it to boot up. After a few minutes, Tim's supervisor said, "It usually doesn't take this long to get started." Tim interpreted this to mean that his supervisor was accusing him of damaging the computer. Tim took the comment personally, when his boss was stating her concern that something might be wrong with the machine.

"Bill doesn't like me," Sharon began, "otherwise why would he make me look bad to the head of the division?"

Bill was Sharon's supervisor. When he promoted Sharon the previous month, he offered her a larger cubicle that was two doors down from his office. Sharon responded to his offer by saying, "Let me think about it." She didn't like change in general and was concerned in particular that the new cubicle would put her within earshot of a co-worker she didn't like.

Four weeks later, Sharon was upset with Bill. "I found out that Mark, the head of the division, asked Bill why I wasn't in the bigger cubicle yet," she explained. "Bill told him 'she doesn't want to move.' That's a lie! I never said that and now Mark will think that I am ungrateful."

Sharon mistakenly assumed Bill's actions as dislike of her. Viewed within the larger context, the events take on a different meaning. For neurotypicals, moving to a larger cubicle that is in closer proximity to a manager is a positive. Bill expected an immediate "yes" from Sharon and had already let Mark know that workspaces would be shifted. As the weeks went on and Sharon continued to ruminate about whether to move, Bill concluded that she really didn't want the new space. When Mark asked him what happened, Bill simply informed him of the situation.

Taking things personally is an example of a cognitive distortion, which is a habitual pattern of negative thinking that results in misreading people and situations. The thoughts associated with cognitive distortion are automatically negative. Something happens and you immediately form a conclusion why, and don't stop to consider whether your conclusion makes sense.

The concept of cognitive distortion was introduced by Dr. David Burns, who authored a classic 1980 book, *Feeling Good: The New Mood Therapy*. A pioneer in the field of cognitive therapy, Burns demonstrated that people can lessen anxiety, depression and other harmful emotions by changing the way they think about events in their lives.

Cognitive distortion is certainly not unique to individuals with Asperger's Syndrome. However, when the negative thought patterns are coupled with impaired theory of mind, a weak drive for central coherence, and anxiety, the potential for misunderstandings are increased.[1]

The most common distorted thinking patterns among my clients are misunderstanding the intentions of others; black & white thinking with no room for compromise or an alternate explanation; and magnifying the severity of a situation. The big clue that perceptions are distorted is the lack of evidence to support them.

Burns described 10 common patterns of distorted thinking. See if you recognize any of them in your thinking.

1. All or nothing thinking: seeing people and situations in absolute terms: good or bad, right or wrong, and smart or stupid.

2. Catastrophizing: the tendency is to exaggerate the potential for negative outcomes. Your boss asks you to redo part of an assignment, and you decide that he's getting ready to fire you.

3. "Shoulds:" a strict set of rules about how people, including yourself, are supposed to act or do things, and exaggerated consequences if a rule is violated. Ellen thinks that colleagues should always meet deadlines or be fired.

4. Personalization: assuming that you are the reason that someone behaved in a certain way without considering other explanations. "Todd didn't say hello to me because he doesn't like me."

5. Jumping to conclusions: *Mind reading,* where you conclude

---

[1] Theory of mind and central coherence are discussed in Chapter 3, Communication Skills at Work.

that someone is reacting negatively to you, without any evidence that this is true ("Dan didn't fix my computer because he wants my projects to be late") or *fortune telling,* anticipating what will go wrong as an established fact.

6. Labeling: assigning negative labels to yourself or other people without having evidence to support that conclusion. "My co-workers are selfish and unsupportive because they wouldn't cover for me;" "The division head is an idiot for not giving me the promotion."

7. Filtering: paying attention only to negative information and filtering out positive information. Jill obsessed over one "needs improvement" in her performance review, and ignored the overall rating of "exceeds expectations" and the recommendation for a raise.

8. Disqualifying positives: insisting that positive experiences don't count, "Anyone could have received the award."

9. Emotional reasoning: the belief that your feelings are the truth. "I feel stupid, so I must be stupid;" "I'm worried about losing my job, so they must be ready to fire me."

10. Overgeneralization: global statements about one-time events. Because you entered one wrong formula into a spreadsheet, you believe that you're no good at budgeting. Or, you get off at the wrong subway stop and believe that you cannot use public transportation.

Changing Distorted Thinking Patterns

"Learn to recognize when your mind is spinning in circles; it is never productive that way."

Industrial Hygienist, age 50

Distorted thinking patterns originate with the thoughts you have about events, not the actual events themselves. The thoughts create feelings which drive actions. Whenever negative thoughts prevent the logical, objective analysis of a situation, conclusions or assumptions become problematic.

Changing distorted thinking patterns is never easy. The effort is worth it if negative thinking is getting in the way of achieving your goals or interacting with others at work.

The first step is to connect your thoughts to the behavior that you want to change. Allison has wanted to find a different job for over two years. Each time she tries to take action, she becomes paralyzed. I asked Allison to write down the thoughts that went through her mind each time she sat down to update her resume. She realized that she focused on an unsuccessful job search experience that happened 5 years earlier. She over-generalized that one experience to mean that, "I'm no good at interviewing, so no one will hire me."

The second step in the change process is to challenge your negative thoughts and replace them with ones that are more realistic and that you believe are true. Take your time with this step. You must believe that your new thoughts are true in order for this technique to work. Allison was able to reframe her thinking and create a new belief: "When I learn new interviewing skills, I can communicate my value to a potential employer."

The Rationality of Beliefs Checklist can help you test the validity of your thought patterns. It is printed on the following page with the kind permission of Dr. Lewis Stern.

When you decide to create a new thought pattern, you need to practice and reinforce it. Allison set a goal of learning how to interview. She started reading books about effective interviewing techniques, and we began role playing interviewing scenarios in our coaching sessions. We placed a special emphasis on communicating how her skills would benefit an employer, and what to do if she was asked a question that she wasn't sure of how to answer. Over the course of a few weeks, Allison's confidence improved and she was able to update her resume.

Here are some suggestions for helping a new thought take root:

- Set a goal based on the new thought pattern and begin taking steps to reach it
- Focus on positive outcomes associated with the new thought
- Repeat the thought silently to yourself as an affirmation
- Write the thought on sticky notes and post them in areas where you will see them throughout the day

Rationality of Beliefs Checklist

When you would like to make sure that specific beliefs you hold or assumptions you have are rational, there are some check-points to help. The following questions can help you explore whether your beliefs or assumptions makes sense, and fit with reality and with what others you respect would think.

For any belief or assumption you want to check for rationality, begin by writing it down. Then answer each of the following ten questions about that belief or assumption. For each question you answer yes, you get one point. When you are done answering the questions, tally your points to see how many of them you get out of ten. The more yes's, the more likely it is that your belief or assumption is rational. The more no's, the more you may want to consider alternative beliefs or assumptions that could help you be more successful, happy, and comfortable with your decisions and actions, and reduce your level of negative stress.

Y N 1. Are you comfortable with the possibility that you may be wrong?

Y N 2. Is this belief/assumption based on an objective view of the facts and does it fit with other relevant facts that you know to be true?

Y N 3. Consider what would happen in the future as a consequence of this belief/assumption. How likely is it that this will actually happen?

Y N 4. Does believing this help protect your life and health?

Y N 5. Do you <u>never</u> deny, exaggerate, or avoid facts or events which may show this to be wrong?

Y N 6. Does this belief/assumption coincide with what you have been told by other people who are usually rational?

Y N 7. Does believing this help you achieve your short- and long-range goals?

Y N 8. When you hear or think of opposing views are you open-minded and willing to consider that they may be true and you may be wrong?

Y N 9. Does believing this help you prevent useless conflict with other people?

Y N 10. Does believing this help you feel the way you need and want to?

(1 point for each yes)   Total: _____ points

Copyright 1979 by Lewis R. Stern. Used with permission.

- Program your computer to send regular emails to yourself that remind you of the change that you are making

To learn more about applying cognitive-behavioral techniques to reduce your levels of stress, I highly recommend *Asperger Syndrome and Anxiety: A Guide to Successful Stress Management,* by Dr. Nick Dubin, who has Asperger's Syndrome.

Managing Anxiety

"I am constantly under a low level of stress, always on the lookout for 'something' to occur, some undefined vague threat. I'm always on guard."

IT Consultant, age 49

Recently, I attended a conference for adults with Asperger's Syndrome. The speaker asked the audience of more than 100 how many had problems with anxiety in their lives. Every single hand went up!

Anxiety is a generalized feeling of "dis-ease" and concern about what might happen in the future. Fear is a reaction to an actual threat. Most of the things people feel anxious about don't actually happen.

Anxiety becomes problematic if it prevents you from approaching co-workers to ask questions, or from carrying out assigned job duties, such as talking to people on the telephone or interacting with customers. One man described his consternation at having to work in a cubicle. The thought of a co-worker entering his space unannounced so unnerved him ("What if I'm asked a question that I'm not prepared to answer?") that he became hypervigilent to the sound of footsteps heading his way.

Severe anxiety can be debilitating and requires medical attention. If you experience mild to moderate anxiety, there are several techniques that can help. Do any of these common anxiety triggers apply to you? You become anxious when:
- Performing a task for the first time
- Recalling a previous bad experience with the same or similar task or situation
- Making, or worrying about making, a mistake

- Not doing perfect work
- Talking to people, in person or via telephone, you don't know
- Having conflicts or disagreement with co-workers
- Not knowing what to say
- Being chastised
- Hearing the judgments of other people
- Facing rejection of yourself or your ideas

No matter what your triggers are, ruminating about what might happen, or what someone might do, wastes energy and leads to more stress.

Andrea began a coaching session panicked about an upcoming meeting. "The vice president wants to discuss the conference that we are holding in a couple of months," she said. "I am terrified about meeting with her! I'll probably say the wrong thing and get fired. I spent almost half an hour in the ladies room crying before I left work to come here."

Andrea was reacting to a potentially stressful situation by making negative assumptions about what could happen. Her thoughts fed a rising feeling of panic that resulted in 30 minutes of tears over something that didn't, and probably wouldn't, occur!

Assumptions are dangerous because they are based on events of long ago that you fear will be repeated in the present. Andrea's assumption was based on her life-long difficulty answering questions spontaneously. "I know what I want to say, but I can't formulate the words," she explained. "I get flustered and blurt out whatever comes to my mind, which usually annoys people."

Andrea's anxiety was understandable. She needed a plan in order to successfully participate in the upcoming meeting. We started gathering factual information instead of relying on assumptions, opinions or guesses.

The facts were: Four people would attend the meeting: Andrea, who handled speaker recruitment; the marketing manager; Andrea's boss, who ran the conference; and the vice president. Andrea had invited the vice president to make a keynote address at the event. The purpose of the meeting was to discuss the topic of the address.

Next, we prepared. Thorough preparation increases confidence and helps people to feel more in control of a situation. Andrea made a list of all the information that she needed to have ready. Since the vice president had only been with the company for 5 months, we anticipated that she would want to learn the history of the event, information about this year's theme, agenda and attendees.

Andrea prepared potential topics for the keynote address, and created a fact sheet with details about the length of the presentation, the audience profile, and information about the venue. We discussed what to do if she was asked a question that she didn't know how to answer. Andrea realized that either her supervisor or the marketing manager would know what to say. "If they don't," she said, "I can tell the vice president that I'll have to research the answer and get back to her."

By this point Andrea was much calmer. My next suggestion was that she practice what she would say at the meeting. She also planned to review her presentation with the marketing manager.

Gathering information, preparation and practice can dramatically lower your levels of anxiety. So can realistic expectations. If you believe that you must do everything perfectly, your anxiety level will be high. But if you shift your focus to doing your best, assisting someone else, or learning a new skill, you will relieve yourself of a lot of pressure.

If you are in the habit, like Andrea, of anticipating negative outcomes, start doing reality checks. Andrea's mind made a huge leap from "meeting with the vice president" to "I'll say the wrong thing and get fired." The next time you catch yourself assuming the worst, ask yourself, "Do I know this is true?" I can confidently predict that 99% of the time your answer will be, "no."

The Possible, Probable, Unlikely Test is another tool for challenging negative, anxiety-provoking thoughts. Begin by writing down the troubling idea or assumption. Ask yourself, "Is it possible?" If the answer is yes, ask, "How probable is it?" If the scenario is likely to happen, ask, "How can I prepare for a better outcome?" If the scenario is unlikely to happen, ask, "What do I need to focus on instead?"

The Possible, Probable, Unlikely Test was used to as a reality check for Andrea's thought, "I'll say the wrong thing and get fired."

- Is it possible? *Yes, there is a possibility that I could say something wrong in the meeting and be fired.*
- How probable is it? *Not very, because everyone makes mistakes. If I make an error, I will say so and find the correct information.*
- What do I need to focus on instead? *Anticipating the questions that will be asked and preparing ahead of time how to answer them.*

When the meeting day arrived, Andrea was able to answer all of the questions posed to her. "I was a little nervous going into the conference room," she said, "but, after a few minutes, I relaxed. I am proud of myself for doing a good job."

Another method for reducing anxiety is reframing. When you reframe a situation, you make a choice to look at it in a different, more positive way. The statement, "No one will hire me because I can't interview well" can be reframed as, "Learning new interviewing skills will enable me to communicate my value to an employer." The statement, "My projects are always late because I'm disorganized" can be reframed as, "My projects will be completed on time when I use better time management techniques."

Many discover that exercise and diet impact their levels of anxiety. A sedentary lifestyle and large amounts of caffeine, sugar, alcohol and processed foods can overexcite the central nervous system which increases stress. Anxiety can be a side effect of some prescription medications. Consult a medical professional to review the effects of the drugs you take.

Sensory Issues on the Job

> "When entering crowded rooms or the cafeteria, the noises I hear are garbled and I can't make sense of them. It all sounds like gibberish."
> **Network Analyst, age 40**

"Can't you ask the cleaning people to vacuum someplace else?" Maura asked, annoyed. I was surprised; I had not been aware that the cleaning crew had started work. Maura's request focused my attention to the hallway outside of my office, where I heard the hum of a vacuum faintly in the background. "I hadn't even noticed it," I said. Maura, incredulous, replied, "It's so loud, I can't concentrate on what you are saying."

Hyper- or hypo-sensitivity to sensory stimuli, or problems processing sensory information, can make concentrating difficult or nearly impossible. Clients describe sneaking into empty conference rooms and making excuses to work at home to avoid being bombarded with overwhelming sights, sounds and smells. Others have found themselves trapped at their desks, tense and unproductive for hours. Still others have devised creative strategies to compensate.

Joseph is an attorney specializing in contract law. "If I look someone in the eye, I can't pay attention to what they are saying," he explained. "So I tell my clients that I need to focus on taking notes when they are talking, in order not to miss any details."

To her embarrassment, Tina often had trouble locating items on her desk. "It's only the ones that are in plain sight," she said facetiously. This problem became worse when she was under a lot of stress. Her solution was to arrange items she used every day alphabetically along her workspace. "Then I know the scissors will be to the left of the stapler."

If your sensory problems are severe, it may be necessary to formally disclose your Asperger's Syndrome to your employer and request accommodations. Otherwise, you might be able to make your needs known without revealing a diagnosis. If you chose this option, plan what you will say so that your employer will understand that this is a real need and not a request for special treatment. One of my clients said to her supervisor, "I need a quiet cubicle so that I can concentrate." She was told, "Everyone wants a quiet cubicle!"

It helps to suggest solutions to your problem. Statements that explain sensitivities and what can be done about them are:

- "I have a photosensitivity to fluorescent lights and need to use a desk lamp instead."

- "The bright light is hurting my eyes. Can we close the blinds?"
- "My hearing is acute and the constant activity around my desk is makes it hard for me to concentrate. Can I move to a space away from the lunch area?"
- "I am having a hard time following everyone's ideas. Can we write them down?"
- "I am hypersensitive to noise and need to wear headphones so that I can concentrate."

There are sensory integration and assistive technologies that can improve your ability to function. Many people who have photosensitivity or other visual processing problems have found success with The Irlen Method (www.irlen.com), which uses colored overlays and filters. Noise-cancelling headphones, like those from Bose Corporation (www.bose.com), and white noise machines are discreet ways to block or reduce background noise. The use of these technologies is becoming more and more common in "cubicle farms" (large open spaces filled with rows of cubicles).

Auditory processing problems can be explained with statements such as, "I have a hearing problem that makes it hard to hear during group discussions." You can request written meeting notes or a debriefing from a colleague. One client was given permission to attend meetings via telephone because the amount of visual and auditory stimulation in a group was overwhelming.

Olfactory sensitivities can be trickier to resolve. It is unlikely that businesses will ban women from wearing perfume or men from using aftershave. However if a particular colleague's fragrance is seriously distracting you, speak to the individual about it. Find a private space, explain the problem and make your request. You can say something like, "I am having an allergic reaction to your perfume. Would you mind not wearing it at the office?" You may also be able to move to a different office, away from the perfume smell.

If the smell of tobacco on the clothes of someone who smokes cigarettes bothers you, try using a plug-in air freshener in your workspace.

Some companies have policies restricting food consumption to the employee cafeteria or lunch room. If your co-workers eat pungent smelling lunches at their desks, discuss this situation with your human resources representative.

 NT TIP: It is considered impolite to make negative comments about the smell, taste or appearance of food that others are consuming.

If your sense of smell is not very sharp, be vigilant about your own use of scented products and your personal hygiene. Dirty clothing carries body odor. I once presented a workshop in a room that was set up for 20 participants. One of the attendees was wearing clothes that were wrinkled, stained and smelly! The odor permeated the room. Some of the other participants stood in the back to avoid sitting near this woman. If you have doubts about your hygiene, ask your work buddy whether you need to make changes and what kind.

Most people with tactile sensitivities are able to find suitable workplace attire because of the variety of fabric choices and the casual dress codes adopted in many companies. Shaking hands can be quite uncomfortable, yet is expected in most business situations. You may be able to desensitize yourself with practice to tolerate a moderate amount of contact. Or, you can feign a mild illness to avoid a handshake ("I think that I am coming down with a cold so I won't shake your hand and give you my germs"), although this will raise suspicion if you do it frequently. Another option is to use your left hand to lightly touch a person's upper right arm as you extend a greeting, "It's nice to meet you!" Keep your right arm by your side and the other person will assume that you are physically unable to shake hands.

You can prepare for indoor temperatures that are too warm or too cold by wearing layers of clothing to put on or take off, and by keeping a sweater at work. Small desk fans and portable space heaters can also help. Check with the office manager to see if there are restrictions on their use.

Some people factor sensory issues into their career choices. Many companies allow employees to work from home offices. Other jobs require a presence in the office, but the employee works in a secluded location away from distractions. Self-employment is yet another option for those who need a controlled environment. This option is not for everyone. Among the drawbacks: the need to actively market your products or services, handle finances (or hire someone to manage them) and an unsteady income.

Dealing with Change

Most people dislike change.

Most people with Asperger's Syndrome dislike change *a lot*. This makes perfect sense. There are so many unknowns in the neurotypical world: why people do things, how you are supposed to behave, what you are supposed to say, what others are thinking, and what people really want. It's only natural that you feel better when your work environment remains stable and predictable.

The problem is that the environment is always changing. Employees leave and new ones are hired to take their place. Individuals get promoted and corporate hierarchies are restructured. Companies are sold, merged and acquired. New technologies can render jobs or processes obsolete. Budgets get cut and business priorities shift.

After 11 years of working together, Richard's supervisor retired. A new manager was hired from another company. Over the next few months, she instituted many changes that affected Richard's job. She expected Richard and his two fellow Web content managers to proofread content, implement search engine optimization strategies, and work with the marketing team to improve product sales. Budget cuts eliminated the freelance help that Richard was accustomed to accessing.

Richard's former supervisor was casual and laid back, his new manager was business-like and demanding. "She thrives on stress," Richard explained, "and stress makes me shut down."

And shut down he did. He began ignoring tasks that he didn't understand. Instead of implementing his manager's suggestions for streamlining his work, Richard continued doing things as he always had. As the stress built, he withdrew into himself, no longer talking to his co-workers. Richard and his new manager became increasingly frustrated with each other. He was given a formal performance improvement plan.

Change can create feelings of uncertainty, anxiety, anger, confusion, fear and sadness. Human beings tend to resist change, by:

- Continuing to work as they have previously
- Refusing to see any benefits of change
- Pointing out why the change won't work
- Incessantly questioning the need for change
- Sabotaging the change with passive-aggressive behaviors like "forgetting" what to do, or acting confused about what needs to happen

Resisting change is ineffective, and can potentially lead to job loss.

Many clients say they were "blindsided" by change (they didn't see it coming). Resignations, layoffs and reorganizations sometimes do occur without warning. Usually, there are signs of a change coming that the person with Asperger's Syndrome doesn't notice.

Industry trends may hint at the possibility of layoffs or even the demise of a company. When multiple firms compete in crowded, mature markets, some will not survive. An aggressive rival or a cutting edge technology can siphon sales and market share, weakening profitability. Regulatory changes dictate how companies in your industry do business. If competitors are outsourcing jobs to cut costs and remain competitive, your company might be forced to do so as well. This is why staying informed about industry trends is a good idea.

When your company's executives have frequent, closed-door meetings, this usually indicates major changes are being planned. The resignations of several executives or department heads can mean your company is in financial difficulty. If consultants have been brought in to review the business, it may be because it will soon be put up for sale. If your supervisor asks frequently for reports about current and projected sales, marketing plans, and expenses, this indicates concerns about losing sales and market share or decreased profitability. A company rumor mill in overdrive often signals changes coming, although what is rumored is not always accurate.

Change can be visible for an employee. Has your manager been preoccupied or spending a lot of time with a peer in your department? Have you been excluded from meetings or pulled off major projects? These can be signs that your manager is getting promoted or leaving the company, that a peer is being groomed for a new role, that a reorganization is taking place, or that your job is in jeopardy.

Do not panic or make assumptions if you suspect change is coming. Talk over the situation with someone you trust, like your work buddy. Do not project your thoughts too far into the future. You may have misread signs or the rumors might be wrong. Continue to do your best and avoid taking part in the rumor mill.

When a change is announced, do not panic or make assumptions, either. Listen carefully to what is said and take notes. People often fear change because they:

- Are uncertain about what to expect from a new manager
- Have concerns about losing their jobs after a company acquisition, merger or sale
- Doubt that a change is needed or desirable
- Believe that there must be negative consequences coming
- Fear that they will lose something of personal value, such as status, power, prestige, authority, security, perks or benefits
- Are afraid to take the risk of learning something new, reporting to a different supervisor or assuming a different role
- Worry they do not possess the knowledge, skills or abilities to succeed in the new environment

Rather than waste your energy resisting the inevitable, take constructive action to adapt. Look for similarities between your work situation before and now. What knowledge, skills and experience can you carry over to the new situation or to a new employer? What can you can do to fit in to new circumstances? If the organization has a new management team or you have a new supervisor, listen carefully to their priorities and goals. If you lack needed skills, come up with a plan for acquiring them.

Ask questions when you are uncertain about what you should do differently. In large group meetings, limit your questions to topics which pertain to the interests of everyone. Save specific concerns about your job for your supervisor.

New managers often ask employees what they would like to change about their jobs or about the company. Frame your responses in a constructive way. Your words and actions are making an impression on people. Negative, judgmental and cynical comments will portray you as an angry, unmotivated employee. Your commitment to the company will be questioned. Compare the following examples of constructive and combative comments:

Combative	*Constructive*
"The sales people are always late turning in their orders and slow down the processing cycle."	"I see some inefficiency between our group and the sales department."
"I am completely bored with my current job."	"I would like to be more involved with the planning of marketing campaigns."
"We've been complaining for months about the outdated order entry system."	"For several months we have been discussing a new order entry system."

Refrain from making disapproving comments about a current or former supervisor, members of the management team or your co-workers. This will have people wondering why *you* can't get along with others. Bottom line: managers want enthusiastic, dedicated people on their team.

Do not resist if you are asked to handle an aspect of your job differently or take on new responsibilities. Treat this as a chance to learn something new that might make your job easier and more interesting. Do not talk about how you used to do things or why the old way was better. It makes you appear unwilling to be a team player.

If you have a new supervisor, pay particular attention to his or her work style. Does he prefer face-to-face meetings or rely mostly on email? Does she like to discuss projects or review written documents? How often does she want to be updated on the status of your projects, and in how much detail? If the answers to these questions are not obvious to you, ask "How would you like me to update you?" or "What is enough detail versus too much?"

Organizations are comprised of groups of people who have disparate backgrounds. They come together for the purpose of contributing their skills to reach a common goal. Cordial and respectful relationships make that process easier and less stressful for everyone.

What to Do If You Are Fired

"University doesn't prepare you for real life work culture."
Administrative Assistant, age 31

Involuntary job loss is a stressful experience that erodes self-confidence and self-esteem. Getting fired ranks 8th out of 43 stressors on the Holmes and Rahe Stress Scale, which measures the impact of various events on an individual's sense of well being.

Job loss is hard on everyone; however persons with Asperger's Syndrome face special challenges. The individual may not really understand why they were terminated, making it difficult to know what to handle differently in the future. There may have been misunderstandings related to theory of mind, pragmatic language, or central coherence that an employer interpreted as behavior problems. Some individuals choose work which emphasizes their challenges, rather than their strengths. Others lack basic job readiness skills that they must master before they are employable.

Whether you have been fired one or multiple times, job loss does not diminish your value as a person. It has to do with your skills and abilities not being the right match for a particular position. What is most important is to learn as much as you can about what went wrong and what changes you need to make.

Even when you didn't enjoy what you were doing, getting fired is a personal loss, and it is normal to feel sadness, anger, confusion, and fear. Find someone to talk to so that you do not become overwhelmed with emotions. Depending on the circumstances of your termination, you may be eligible to collect unemployment insurance. Check with your state unemployment office.

There are some lucky individuals who receive specific feedback about why they were let go. I say 'lucky' because they know what areas they need to develop. Most are given vague reasons that are hard to act on ("not being a team player," "hard to get along with").

It is sometimes possible to contact a former supervisor or a former colleague to clarify why you were let go. This should be done to find out what you need to correct, not to argue for why you should get your job back. Initiate the contact within one week of being terminated, via telephone or email. *Do not* visit your former place of employment without prior approval. If your request is denied, accept it and do not ask again. If your job ended after much conflict, it is best not to contact anyone in the company, unless it is to discuss an administrative issue concerning health insurance benefits, unemployment claims, or a final pay check. Contact the human resources department about this issue.

These are some common reasons that people with Asperger's Syndrome lose their jobs, and suggestions about skills that you may need to develop (which have been discussed in previous chapters).

EMPLOYER SAID THAT YOU WERE RUDE, DIFFICULT TO WORK WITH, NOT A TEAM PLAYER:
» Focus on your communication skills, particularly small talk, to form good working relationships. Understand what topics are considered controversial or polarizing so that you avoid them at work. "Difficult to work with" might mean that you continually challenged the ideas of other people, didn't listen to instructions or follow procedures, or did not accept

feedback or criticism. It is a reality of the workplace that people need to function well in groups.

YOU THOUGHT THAT EVERYTHING WAS FINE AND WERE COMPLETELY SHOCKED TO BE FIRED:

» It is likely that you missed signs that there were problems with your performance. Most NTs are completely unaware that some people have trouble with non-verbal communication or take language very literally, missing the implied meaning. They assume that you understand things as they do. In the future, clarify assignments and check in with your supervisor at regular intervals to review your performance. Ask peers for ideas about how to be more efficient on the job. If you frequently hear phrases like, "you shouldn't have to ask that;" "we went through this already;" "you didn't listen;" you are being told that you are not meeting your employer's expectations.

YOU LOST YOUR TEMPER, SAID OR DID INAPPROPRIATE THINGS, HAD CONFLICTS WITH YOUR SUPERVISOR OR CO-WORKERS:

» It is my experience that these are chronic problems that usually result in multiple job losses. You must learn to manage your anger, frustration and stress. Think seriously about your career choice: are you a field that is too demanding or that requires too much interaction with others? Perhaps you have unrealistic expectations about your decision making or other authority. Do you feel contempt for people who you believe are not as intelligent as you are? Working well with others is almost always more important than raw intellect for career success.

YOU WERE BORED OR UNHAPPY WITH YOUR WORK AND STOPPING TRYING, BECAME CHRONICALLY LATE, OR REFUSED TO FOLLOW INSTRUCTIONS:

» Termination is never desirable because it creates a situation that must be explained during job interviews. If you are unable to continue in a job, resign and give your employer a minimum of two week's notice before you leave. No matter what your personal feelings are about the company or the people in it, do your best to leave on good terms. That means acknowledging that things did not work out and leaving without incident. You never know when you might work with someone again, or need a reference.

THE QUALITY OF YOUR WORK WAS FINE, BUT YOU WERE UNABLE TO MEET PRODUCTIVITY REQUIREMENTS:

- » Review the project planning and time management tips in the section on executive function. Think about whether you spent too much time on non-essential tasks, or re-inventing the wheel instead of following established procedures. Perhaps trying to make every project "perfect" ate up time that should have been spent on other priorities. At your next job, find a work buddy who can help you understand what is expected. If you have lost more than one job due to productivity issues, you may be in the wrong kind of work environment. Are you choosing jobs in companies or industries that are known for high pressure and tight deadlines, such as venture capital-backed start-ups? In what type of work environment could you best apply your skills?

YOU WERE CONFUSED ABOUT EXPECTATIONS, ASKED TOO MANY OR TOO FEW QUESTIONS, AND DID NOT TAKE INITIATIVE:

- » Learn how to clarify the expectations about your job performance and how assignments should be completed. If anxiety prevents you from asking questions or carrying out particular tasks, take steps to manage it, seeking medical help if necessary. Ask what you should do next once assigned tasks are finished. Being idle is associated with laziness or low motivation.

If you have had continual problems maintaining employment, you may need to train for different work. Find a professional such as a career counselor or coach who can help you to figure out what your talents and skills are, and what careers you might enjoy. If possible, train for a field that is growing and in need of workers. Employers in need of skilled employees may be more willing to overlook a spotty background.

What NOT To Do if You are Fired

Matt contacted me in an emotional roil. After weeks of conflict with his supervisor, he had been fired. In frustration and anger, he had yelled in the hallways about how unfair his boss and the company had been to him. He threatened to contact a lawyer to discuss suing the firm. Matt was escorted from the building by security personnel. He wanted my opinion about his plan to picket the company for depriving him of a livelihood.

We discussed how picketing the company would alienate his former colleagues—whom he would need for future references. It might also lead to his arrest. Any negative publicity would cause other companies to avoid hiring him.

To my relief, Matt ended the call by thanking me for helping him see that picketing the company would be a huge mistake that could negatively affect his career for years to come.

Matt's situation illustrates why it is never a good idea to act when your emotions are running high. Strong emotions can literally prevent you from thinking clearly. Difficult as it may be, accept the news of termination quietly. Vent your emotions privately, away from the workplace. Do not take any action until you are calm. Discuss the situation, and what to do next, with someone you know and trust.

CHAPTER EIGHT

In the Final Analysis

It is my prediction that by 2013, Asperger's Syndrome will be as well known by the general public as AD/HD is now in 2010. That estimate appears to be accurate. Prime time network television programs, such as NBC's *Parenthood,* have characters with Asperger's Syndrome. Tim Page, a Pulitzer Prize-winning music critic, scored a best-seller with his memoir, *Parallel Play,* which recounts growing up with undiagnosed Asperger's Syndrome. Specialisterne, the Danish software testing company that hires people on the autism spectrum, is featured in a Harvard Business School case study.[1] The HBO film, *Temple Grandin,* won seven awards at the 62nd annual Emmy Awards. In June, 2010 Ari Ne'eman, Founding President of the Autistic Self Advocacy Network, became the first autistic person appointed to the National Council on Disability.

The business community in the United States has been slower to recognize the Aspergians in their midst, although awareness is increasing. In Illinois, Aspiritech (www.aspiritech.org) has adapted the Specialisterne model and trains individuals with Asperger's and high functioning autism to test software for their client companies. In 2008, Symmetry Electronics partnered with F.A.C.T, a Los Angeles non-profit, in a program to match the skills of adults on the autism spectrum with the needs of employers. In a press release on the Symmetry Electronics Web site Gil Zaharoni, CEO, says, "The launch of our program has been a great success ... The employees that we hired as a result are extremely talented and bright individuals and have become valuable assets to Symmetry."

---

[1] *Specialisterne: Sense & Details,* by Robert D. Austin, Jonathan Wareham, Javier Busquets, Copyright ©2008 President and Fellows of Harvard College.

More such efforts, in both the for- and non-profit sectors, are bound to follow. It is currently estimated that 1 in 110 children are diagnosed with an autism spectrum disorder.[2] Creating opportunities for them to secure meaningful employment when they grow up benefits both the individuals, and employers in need of skilled, loyal workers.

Until the day that "Aspie-friendly" companies become the norm rather than the exception, the burden is on you to fit in. Continue to develop your skills and abilities. Research which jobs and work environments are a good match. If something doesn't work out, learn from it and move on to something else. Be willing to try some of the techniques that are explained in this book, as they have helped others improve their employment experiences.

In closing, I offer a bit of levity with my version of the famous "Final Analysis" prayer that is attributed to Mother Theresa.

> *NTs are often unreasonable, illogical and social. Forgive and make small talk with them anyway.*
>
> *If you try to be friendly and socialize, NTs may accuse you of being rude, nasty or difficult to work with. Be friendly anyway.*
>
> *If you are successful, NTs may assume that you work in engineering or computers. Succeed anyway.*
>
> *If you are honest, NTs will be insulted. Be honest anyway (except when discussing a woman's hairstyle, weight or clothing).*
>
> *The perfect, detailed systems you spend years creating, NTs can destroy overnight. Create anyway.*
>
> *If you find serenity and happiness indulging your special interest in washing machines, string theory or the migratory patterns of Altai Mountain Yaks, NTs may be jealous. Keep indulging anyway.*
>
> *The errors you point out today, NTs will soon forget. Point them out anyway.*

---

[2] *DCD Study: An average of 1 in 110 Children have [sic] an ASD,* Centers for Disease Control, www.cdc.gov.

Give your best at multitasking, and it will never be fast enough. So concentrate on one thing at a time instead.

Because in the final analysis, it is between you and your affinity for logic and analysis. It was never between you and NTs anyway.

APPENDIX *(This section may be photocopied for distribution.)*

Asperger's Syndrome Guide for Employers

Asperger's Syndrome is a neurobiological disorder that affects an individual's ability to read and respond to social cues, communicate effectively, and organize and prioritize tasks. The individual may make blunt or inappropriate comments, and have difficulty multitasking and seeing the big picture. He or she may be unusually distracted by noise, smells and/or physical sensations and have problems with fine and gross motor skills.

Although only officially recognized by the medical community in 1994, the prevalence of Asperger's Syndrome is estimated to be as high as 1 in every 250 people in the United States.[1] At the time of this writing, theories about its etiology and the diagnostic criteria continue to evolve. It is generally agreed that Asperger's Syndrome is a mild form of autism.

It is important to remember that "when you've met one person with Asperger's Syndrome, you've met one person with Asperger's Syndrome." Each individual is unique and does not share all of the features of Asperger's or experience them to the same degree. In my coaching practice, I work with individuals who need significant support to hold any job, and those who are employed at major corporations and earning six-figure salaries.

While these individuals face a number of challenges, Asperger's Syndrome also confers specific strengths that make them particularly well-suited to jobs requiring attention to detail and prolonged focus. Many have above-average or superior intelligence and enter the

---
[1] *The Complete Guide to Asperger's Syndrome,* ©2007 Tony Attwood, Jessica Kingsley Publishers.

workforce with advanced or multiple degrees. Although having employment in all job levels and business sectors, the fields of computer technology, academic and scientific research, writing, engineering, technical documentation, and academia make particularly good use of their logic and analytical skills.

Differences in the way that the Asperger's brain processes information can be a terrific asset to the business community when individuals are placed in the right jobs and receive the right supports. Specialisterne is a for-profit software testing company that specifically hires individuals with Asperger's Syndrome in order to utilize their unique cognitive abilities. Based in Denmark, its clients include Microsoft, Oracle and CSB. According to founder Thorkil Sonne, Asperger's employees make superior software testers because, "...they are methodical and exhibit great attention to detail" and have "motivation, focus, persistence, precision and ability to follow instructions."[2]

In the United States, Aspiritech has adapted the Specialisterne model and trains individuals with Asperger's Syndrome and high functioning autism to test software for their client companies (learn more at www.aspiritech.org).

The strengths of individuals with Asperger's Syndrome include:
- Attention to detail and sustained concentration which result in accurate, high-quality work
- Excellent long-term memory and recall of facts and details
- Tolerance of repetition and routine
- Strong logic and analytic skills
- Vast knowledge of specialized fields
- Ability to think outside the box
- Absence of social filtering (will say when the emperor has no clothes!)
- Perseverance
- Honesty and loyalty

---

[2] *"Specialisterne finds a place in workforce for people with autism,"* by Cliff Saran, ComputerWeekly.com, February 8, 2008, Reed Business Information.

Common Workplace Challenges

Individuals with Asperger's Syndrome vary widely in their abilities, challenges and need of support. Some appear awkward in their interactions with others, forgetting to make eye contact or to smile, or talking too loudly, softly or quickly. Others are charming and talkative, but may ask too many questions, or alienate others with quirky behavior or social gaffes. Still others confound colleagues with an apparent lack common sense or unusual naiveté.

Workplace challenges fall into three main categories: social and communication skills, planning and organization, and sensory/motor issues. As expected, communication presents a significant hurdle. Often, the social and communication difficulties of people with Asperger's Syndrome appear to be attitude or behavior problems.

SOCIAL AND COMMUNICATION CHALLENGES

Many Asperger's individuals equate navigating in the business social world with being in a foreign culture. Imagine how hard it would be to communicate if you couldn't tell whether someone's facial expression or tone of voice was happy, sad, or mad. Or if you took language very literally and thought that having a "bad hair day" at work was a grooming issue. Or if looking someone in the eye was distracting or painful. Imagine how excruciating it would be if you didn't know how to make small talk or casual conversation during a lunch break.

Their difficulty understanding non-verbal communication means that Asperger's individuals struggle to make sense of about 93% of human interaction! This is because only 7% of meaning comes from spoken words. About 70% comes from body language, such as a facial expression, gestures and physical proximity to someone else. The remaining 23% comes from vocal tone, volume, inflection and rate of speech. Most people learn how to interpret non-verbal communication intuitively as young children. People with Asperger's Syndrome must learn these skills intellectually.

An individual's theory of mind skills also impact communication.

Theory of mind is the ability to recognize that other people have thoughts, desires, knowledge and motives that differ from yours. It is what enables you to make educated guesses about how someone else will respond to a situation, what they are feeling or what they would like you to do. Individual's with Asperger's Syndrome often have trouble identifying the expectations, motives and needs of others, unless they are explicitly stated. They respond to situations based upon their point of view.

The drive for central coherence, or to see "the big picture," is another factor in human interaction. Most people unconsciously analyze a situation by noticing relevant information from the environment, and recalling similar events from the past. Irrelevant details are filtered out. Individuals with Asperger's Syndrome notice many details, and have trouble distinguishing which are important and not. They must piece together a plethora of facts one by one until the big picture emerges. Central coherence is involved in planning and organization, and helps a person decide how to respond appropriately to a situation.

Difficulty understanding non-verbal communication, seeing another person's perspective, and focusing on the big picture means that a person with Asperger's Syndrome may:

- Take language literally and miss nuances, such as implied meanings or sarcasm
- Make statements that are too honest and direct, unintentionally offending others
- Neglect to make eye contact or to smile
- Not know how to make "small talk" and appear disinterested or unfriendly
- Talk at length about areas of interest and not notice that others want to end the conversation
- Speak to a supervisor in the same way they would speak to a peer
- Interrupt; talk too quickly/slowly; too loudly/softly
- End conversations by simply walking away

Organizational Challenges

Organizing information, planning tasks and prioritizing are executive functions of the brain. These are the skills that enable a person to manage their time and resources efficiently, monitor situations, predict likely outcomes, make good decisions and change course when necessary. People with Asperger's Syndrome have varying degrees of difficulty with executive functions and may need assistance organizing their time and projects.

Difficulty with executive functions means that a person with Asperger's Syndrome may:

- Have trouble getting started on assignments
- Not know how long a project or task will or should take
- Focus too much on details
- Have trouble developing alternatives
- Need explicit direction about what the finished product should look like
- Require written instructions and notes
- Need help prioritizing tasks
- Have difficulty multitasking
- Appear not to take initiative, because they don't know what needs to be done next
- Ask too many questions in an attempt to clarify assignments or expectations
- Act impulsively, or based on too little information
- Resist change

Sensory Challenges

Due to brain processing anomalies, people with Asperger's Syndrome may experience extreme sensitivities to light, sound, smells, and touch (such as the feel of certain fabrics on the skin). Some individuals can actually see the cycling of fluorescent lights, or hear a co-worker's typing as a cacophony of utterly distracting noise.

Auditory processing problems can make it hard for them to understand spoken directions and follow group conversations. The individual may not recognize that he or she is speaking too loudly, too softly or in a monotone.

Sensory issues can make it difficult or impossible for some individuals to pay attention to input from multiple sensory channels at once, such as making eye contact and listening to what someone is saying. Visual-spatial problems may make it hard to locate items on a desk, or to notice that they are standing too close to others.

There may also be difficulties with fine and gross motor skills. The individual might not be able to write legibly or fold and stuff papers neatly into an envelope. The person might be clumsy or have an awkward gait.

Difficulty with sensory and motor abilities means that a person with Asperger's Syndrome may:

- Require a quiet workspace
- Need a natural light source or incandescent light bulbs
- Wear noise-cancelling headphones or use a white noise machine
- Need breaks to avoid sensory overload
- Work in an environment free of perfumes and other scents
- Participate in meetings via telephone

Optimal Jobs & Work Environments

Asperger's Syndrome exists on a spectrum and individuals can vary widely in their abilities and challenges. However generalities can be made about the kinds of jobs and work environments that are most conducive to their success.

Difficult jobs/work environments tend to be those that:
- Require multitasking or responding to frequent interruptions
- Involve quick decision making
- Are high pressure

- Are unstructured and rapidly changing
- Require lots of social interaction
- Involve managing other people
- Demand high rates of speed

Optimal jobs/work environments tend to be those that:
- Allow concentration on one task at a time
- Require accuracy and quality versus speed
- Offer structure and clear performance expectations
- Have at least some elements of routine
- Require minimal social interaction or scripted interaction
- Do not involve the management of others

Working with People Who Have Asperger's Syndrome

There are a number of things that employers can do to help individuals with Asperger's Syndrome to be productive and successful at their jobs. If you know or suspect that someone has Asperger's Syndrome:

- Be patient with training and break instruction into small segments. If an individual is asking an excessive number of questions it could indicate anxiety or confusion about an assignment.

- Provide specific, quantifiable expectations: "the draft is due in 3 days and should include at least 6 ideas for improving efficiency" or "30 entries or more must be made per hour."

- Give regular, specific feedback about performance, since the individual may not notice non-verbal signals that they are not meeting expectations.

- Encourage the use of checklists, electronic reminders, and a personalized "rule book" of processes, procedures and where to go for help. Providing written instructions and color-coded filing systems can help them organize information more efficiently.

- Be mindful that usually what looks like a behavior or attitude problem is a communication problem. The individual often doesn't know that they have offended or angered a colleague.

APPENDIX: ASPERGER'S GUIDE FOR EMPLOYERS

- Don't take blunt remarks or social gaffes personally; use clarifying questions to understand the individual's intentions. Be specific and matter-of-fact in pointing out inappropriate or unacceptable behavior. General statements such as "You're rude," "You're not a team player," or "How could you say that?!" are confusing. Be direct: "When you tell people to 'be quiet' it's considered rude. Instead, ask them to lower their voices."

- Assign a "work buddy" or mentor to explain social norms, encourage social interaction and answer questions. People with Asperger's Syndrome may hesitate to ask questions out of fear that they will appear "stupid." This is likely a by-product of being bullied or ostracized in school.

- Relaxed standards for "teamwork" can be an effective, zero-cost accommodation for people who struggle with social interaction. Allow these individuals to focus on the technical aspects of the job.

- Educate human resources personnel, managers and employees about Asperger's Syndrome. Increased understanding is directly proportional to increased employment success. Retaining just one employee at risk of derailing more than covers the investment in training.

- Provide a coach who is familiar with conditions like Asperger's Syndrome to work with an employee and his or her manager. The pragmatic, goal-oriented nature of the coaching, combined with an action plan based on organizational and individual needs, assures that performance objectives are addressed. (Although it is illegal under the Americans with Disabilities Act to ask an employee about a disability, you *can* discuss performance issues.)

Excerpted from the *Asperger's Syndrome Workplace Survival Guide*, © 2010 Barbara Bissonnette, Forward Motion Coaching (www.ForwardMotion.info).

BIBLIOGRAPHY

Attwood, Tony. *The Complete Guide to Asperger's Syndrome*. London: Jessica Kingsley Publishers, 2007.

Austin, Robert D., Jonathan Wareham, and Javier Busquets. "*Specialisterne: Sense & Details.*" Harvard Business Review (Harvard Business School Press), February, 2008 (President and Fellows of Harvard College).

Baker, Dr. Jed. *The Social Skills Picture Book for High School and Beyond*. Arlington, TX: Future Horizons, Inc., 2006.

Barron, Sean, Dr. Temple Grandin. *Unwritten Rules of Social Relationships, Decoding Social Mysteries Through the Unique Perspective of Autism*. Arlington, TX: Future Horizons, Inc., 2005.

Block, Peter. *Flawless Consulting, A Guide to Getting Your Expertise Used. Second Edition*. San Francisco, CA: Jossey-Bass/Pfeiffer, A Wiley Company, 1981 and 2000.

CDC study: *An average of 1 in 110 children have an ASD. Centers for Disease Control and Prevention*. 2010. www.cdc.gov/Features/Countingautism (accessed 2010 August).

Dubin, Nick. *Asperger Syndrome and Anxiety, A Guide to Successful Stress Management*. London: Jessica Kingsley Publishers, 2009

Electronics, Symmetry. *Symmetry Electronics Starts Outreach Program Employing Adults with Autism*. September 2, 2008. www.symmetryelectronics.com/pages/asp/Press.asp?id=83.

Fast, Yvona. *Employment for Individuals with Asperger Syndrome or Non-Verbal Learning Disability*. London: Jessica Kingsley Publishers, 2004.

Gabor, Don. *How to Start a Conversation and Make Friends*. New York, NY: A Fireside Book, Published by Simon & Schuster, 1983, 2001.

Gaus, Valerie L. *Cognitive-Behavioral Therapy for Adult Asperger Symdrome*. New York, NY: The Guilford Press, 2007.

Goleman, Daniel. *Working with Emotional Intelligence*. New York, NY: Bantam Books, 1998.

BIBLIOGRAPHY

Grandin, Temple, and Kate Duffy. *Developing Talents, Careers for Individuals with Asperger Syndrome and High-Functioning Autism.* Shawnee Mission, KS: Autism Asperger Publishing Company, 2008.

Greater Washington Educational Telecommunications Association, Inc. www.ldpride.net (accessed 2010).

Holmes, Thomas H., and Richard H. Rahe. *"The Holmes and Rahe Stress Scale, Understanding the Impact of Long-Term Stress."* Mind Tools Limited. 1995 -- 2010. www.mindtools.com (accessed September 2010).

Lewis, Michael. *The Big Short: Inside the Doomsday Machine.* New York, NY: W.W. Norton & Company, 2010.

Lovett, Juanita P., Ph.D. *Solutions for Adults with Asperger Syndrome, Maximizing the Benefits, Minimizing the Drawbacks to Achieve Success.* Gloucester, MA: Fair Winds Press, 2005.

McIntyre, Marie G., Ph.D. *Secrets to Winning at Office Politics.* New York: St. Martin's Press, 2005.

Meltzer, Lynn. *Executive Function Education from Theory to Practice.* Edited by Lynn Meltzer. New York, NY: The Guilford Press, 2007.

Palladino, Lucy Jo, Ph.D. *Find Your Focus Zone, An Effective New Plan to Defeat Distraction and Overload.* New York, NY: Free Press, A Division of Simon & Shuster, Inc., 2007.

Peltier, Bruce, Ph.D., M.B.A. *The Psychology of Executive Coaching, Theory and Application.* New York, NY: Taylor & Francis Group, 2001.

Saran, Cliff. *Specialisterne finds a place in workforce for people with autism.* Reed Business Information. February 8, 2008. www.computerweekly.com (accessed April 2008).

Ward, Sarah. *"How to Teach Executive Function Skills at Home."* Lincoln, MA: The Center for Executive Function Skill Development, 2009.

Winner, Michelle Garcia, and Pamela Crooke. *Socially Curious and Curiously Social, A Social Thinking Guidebook for Teens & Young Adults with Asperger's, ADHD, PDD-NOS, NVLD, or other Murky Undiagnosed Social Learning Issues.* San Jose, CA: Think Social Publishing, Inc., 2009.

Zaks, Zosia. *Life and Love: Positive Strategies for Autistic Adults.* Shawnee Mission, KS: Autism Asperger Publishing Company, 2006.

About the Author

Barbara Bissonnette is a certified coach and the Principal of Forward Motion Coaching (www.ForwardMotion.info). She specializes in career development coaching and workplace advocacy for individuals with Asperger's Syndrome and Nonverbal Learning Disorder. She also consults with employers so that they can utilize the skills of employees with social, communication and executive function challenges.

Prior to coaching, Barbara spent more than 20 years in business, most recently as Vice President of Marketing and Sales for an information services company. She has experience hiring and managing people at all levels. She also understands the challenges of Asperger's Syndrome and NLD and focuses on practical strategies for employment success.

Barbara earned a graduate certificate in Executive Coaching from the Massachusetts School Professional Psychology and is certified by the Institute for Professional Empowerment Coaching.

She has spoken about Asperger's Syndrome and employment at Antioch University, Asperger's Association of New England (AANE), Bentley College, Central Massachusetts Employer's Association, Community Resources for People with Autism, Emerson Hospital, Katherine Greer Associates, Massachusetts School of Professional Psychology, New England Human Resources Association, Rhode Island Psychological Association, Shriver Job Corp, and The Wellness Corporation. Her articles have been published in *Insights* magazine, *Austim-Asperger's Digest Magazine*, Autism Family Online and the *AANE Journal*.

INDEX

A

Anxiety
    Asperger Syndrome and Anxiety, 129
    Assumptions and, 130
    Diet and, 132
    Expectations and, 131
    Managing, 131
    Reframing, 132
    Triggers, 129-130
Asperger's Syndrome Guide for Employers, 148
Aspiritech, 145, 149
Authority
    Dealing with, 80-82
    Office politics, 66, 67
    Over-stepping, 75

B

Big picture, 31, 33, 34, 51, 67, 83, 96, 98, 118, 120
Body language
    Communication challenge, 114, 150
    Communicating with, 41-42
    Your own, 43
Burry, Michael, 56

C

Career
    Choosing the right, 8-9
    Informational interviews, 15-22
    Managing, 54-55
    Researching, 10-15
Central coherence
    Cognitive distortion and, 125
    Communication and, 33, 151
    Definition of, 33-34

Change
    Adapting to, 139-140
    Fears of, 138
    Resisting, 137
    Signs of, 137-138
Cognitive distortion
    Frustration and, 123
    Negative thoughts, 124, 126, 127
    Patterns of Distorted Thinking, 125
    Rationality of Beliefs Checklist, 128
    Taking comments personally, 123, 124
Communication skills
    Advance planning, 37
    Checklist of common challenges, 114
    Emotions and, 31
    Good enough, 30, 31
    Social context and, 33
    Teamwork and, 52
    Understanding expectations and, 98
Conflict
    How to handle, 72-77
    Job loss and, 142
    Teams and, 50
    With authority, 80-82
Context
    Communication, 37
    Misunderstandings, 76
    Pragmatics, 33
    Situational, 96, 123, 124
Corporate culture, 11, 65, 71
Criticism
    Accepting, 78, 79, 80
    Difference from feedback, 78-79

D

Decision making
    Authority and, 142
    Emotional overwhelm and, 120
    Flexibility and, 89
    Processing speed and, 90

Disclosure
    Accommodations, 102, 108-109, 110-111
    Americans with Disabilities Act, 107
    Asperger's Syndrome Guide for Employers, 148
    Checklist of common challenges, 114-115
    Disclosure strategy, 111-115
    Essential job functions, 109-110
    Examples of disclosure, 116-119
Discrepancy analysis, 24
Disagreement, see Conflict

E

Elevator speech, 62-63
Emotions
    Amygdala hijack, 120
    Big picture and, 31
    Body language, 41
    Cognitive distortion and, 125
    Neurotypical communication and, 31
    Stress and, 120
    Triggers, 121
Executive function
    Action plan, 104-105
    Definition of, 83-84, 152
    Estimating time, 87
    Project planning, 86-88
    SMART Goals, 103-104
    (See also Decision making, Expectations, Flexibility, Multitasking, Options, Time management, Processing speed, Working memory)
Expectations
    Meeting employer's, 97-101, 142, 143
    Unrealistic, 25, 123, 131, 142

F

Feedback
    Giving, 75, 76-77
    Meeting expectations, 99
    Receiving, 77-8-; 142
    Work buddy and, 49
Fired, see Job loss

Flexibility
    Decision making and, 89
    Increasing mental, 89-90
Frustration
    Cognitive distortion and, 123
    Emotional challenge, 115
    Reasonable goals and, 104
    Triggers, 121

G

Getting hired
    Impediments to, 22-28

H

Help
    Asking for, 93-96
    Giving, 96-97
    Holmes and Rahe Street Scale, 140

I

Informational interviews, 15-22
Intentions of others, misunderstanding and, 125
Interest inventories, 12
Interrupting, 40, 51, 122
Interviews
    Disclosure and, 109
    Tips for, 28-29

J

Job loss
    Emotions and, 141
    Reasons for, 141-143
Job shadowing, 14-15
Judgment, see Feedback

L

Learning style, 102
LinkedIn, 16, 20, 61, 106

Listening
    Active listening, 40
    Auditory learning, 102
    Right impression, 40
    Teamwork, 50, 51

M

Multitasking
    Career choice, 14, 24, 25
    Definition of, 84-85
    Processing speed and, 90
    Working memory and, 85

N

Networking
    Elevator speech and, 62-63
    Finding work and, 25
    How to, 60-63
    Informational interviewing and, 16, 20, 22
Neurotypical
    Assumptions of, 142
    Big picture thinking, 98
    Definition of, 3
    Emotions and communication, 31
    Multitasking and, 56
    Social orientation, 30-31
    Workplace, success in, 81
Nonverbal communication, 33, 39, 41, 42
NT, *see Neurotypical*

O

Occupational Outlook Handbook, 13
Office politics, 48, 64-72
O*Net, 13
Options, 36, 37, 84, 89, 91

P

Pragmatics, 33
Processing speed
    Compensating for slow, 90-91
    Decision making and, 90
    Multitasking and, 90
    Workplace accommodations, 117

Q

Questions
    Anticipating, 132
    Asking too many, 93, 94, 100
    Disability-related from employers, 109
    Email and, 92
    Informational interviews, at, 21
    Job interviews, at, 28-29
    New on job and, 94
    Situational context and, 37
    Slow processing and, 90, 111, 122
    Who to ask, 94, 95, 99

R

Resume, 22, 25, 26-27, 29, 113

S

Scripts, 31
Sensory challenges
    Assistive technologies, 134
    At work, 133-136, 152-153
    Irlen Method, The, 134
    Personal hygiene, 135
Small talk, 38, 44-46, 141
Specialisterne, 56, 113, 145, 149
Strengths
    Asperger mind, 55-56
    Building, 58
    Negotiating tool, 57
    Skills and, 57
    Talents and, 57
Stress
    Amygdala hijack, 120
    Emotional triggers, 120
    Physical signals of, 122
    Strategies to reduce, 122-123

T

Team player
    How to be, 50-53
    Job loss and, 140-141
    Promotions and, 69

Teamwork
    Company culture, 52
    Job qualifications, 24
    Job research, 14
Theory of Mind
    Cognitive distortion and, 125
    Decisions and, 35
    Definition of, 34, 150-151
    Increasing skills in, 37
    Time management, 91-93, 143

W

Work buddy, 47-50, 71, 77, 80, 95, 96, 135, 138, 143
Work environment
    Change and, 136
    Job loss and, 143
    Office politics, 72
    Success at work, 8, 11
Working memory, 84-86
Working with Emotional Intelligence, 120